Reprogrammed

Reprogrammed

How Your Apps, Maps, and Feeds Quietly Shape Your Choices

Rowan Hale

Mindful Pages

Published in 2025

ISBN: 9789371779456 (PB)
ISBN: 9789371777865 (eBook)

Published by

Mindful Pages
Imprint of Alpha Editions LLC
312 W. 2nd St #1834
Casper, WY 82601, USA

This book was developed using advanced writing tools to support the drafting and ideation process. All content has been thoughtfully curated, refined, and reviewed to ensure quality and relevance.

Content

Introduction
The New Architecture of Choice

You pick up your phone. A notification draws your attention to a headline you never sought. A map app presents the fastest route without a thought from you. Your feed scrolls endlessly, offering content that feels tailored, yet may be training your preferences more than reflecting them. Each gesture seems effortless, each choice seamless. In truth, no choice is being made by you alone.

Every day, in ways so subtle they almost escape notice, digital systems shape what we see, what we consider, and even what we believe. These platforms are far from passive instruments awaiting command; they are active environments, engineered to guide attention, foreground certain outcomes, and conceal alternatives. There is no coercion, no overt trickery. The influence is woven into defaults, suggestions, interface cues, and algorithmic scaffolding, quietly shaping action before awareness catches up.

This is not merely a tale of technology in the abstract. It is a story about the architecture of your daily life—how devices, apps, feeds, and maps choreograph where you go, what you do, and, perhaps most insidiously, who you perceive yourself to be. Reprogrammed examines this unseen design, the infrastructure that moves our decisions from deliberate acts to nearly invisible management.

Much has been written about digital distraction, misinformation, and eroded attention spans. These are real, pressing problems. Yet they are symptoms. The root lies deeper: in the very mechanics of modern interfaces, in the seamless automation that manages choice itself. When a route is optimised, a feed curated, and an ad personalised, the promise of convenience masks a subtler reality—a system of influence embedded into the ordinary, shaping behaviour in ways we rarely notice.

The question this book poses is neither nostalgic nor conspiratorial. It is practical, immediate, and vital: how do we tell the difference between a decision we genuinely make and one quietly made for us?

To answer this, we must move past vague hand-waving about "the algorithm" or generic complaints about information overload. This is not an alarmist tract, nor a call for digital retreat. It is an exploration of design as behavioural architecture—how systems ostensibly built to serve have also begun to guide, often imperceptibly. Preserving agency demands more than awareness; it requires fluency: the capacity to read these systems, understand their logics, and intervene in ways that restore deliberation, intention, and genuine choice.

The Illusion of Seamlessness

Design has always shaped behaviour. The placement of a staircase can encourage movement; the shape of a table can invite conversation or silence it. But in the digital domain, design has taken on a more sophisticated, and more elusive, role. Interfaces are no longer static—they are dynamic, reactive, and often predictive. They respond to your gestures, learn from your inputs, and adapt to your routines. They do not merely present options; they suggest which ones to prefer.

This seamlessness is the genius—and the danger—of modern digital environments. It flatters us into thinking we are in charge, even as the system does the steering. When your streaming service queues up the next episode, when your GPS defaults to a certain route, when your feed withholds certain stories in favour of others, you are not encountering neutrality. You are encountering intention—designed, often profit-driven, sometimes benign, but rarely transparent.

And because these systems are so well integrated into our routines, their influence becomes background noise. We don't question the feed; we consume it. We don't examine the route; we follow it. We assume the convenience we're offered is synonymous with our own best interest.

Architecture, Not Accident

It is tempting to believe that these shifts are accidental—that they emerge organically from technical progress or user demand. But the truth is more complex. Each swipe, click, or scroll is undergirded by layers of decisions made by product designers, behavioural economists, data scientists, and machine learning models. Their work is not neutral—it encodes preferences, assumptions, and incentives. It reflects what platforms want users to do, what advertisers want to sell, and what engineers want to optimise.

This is not a conspiracy. It's a business model.

But the result is the same: a behavioural environment in which we are constantly responding to systems that have pre-configured our responses. We are not mindless, nor are we helpless—but we are being shaped. And until we see the shape, we cannot resist it.

This book invites you to look directly at that shape.

Beyond Awareness: Towards Agency

We have entered an age in which behavioural engineering has become infrastructural. Your choices are being scaffolded by systems designed to maximise engagement, minimise friction, and predict your next move. Some of these optimisations are genuinely helpful. Others, less so. The critical point is not to vilify these systems, but to interrogate them—because in doing so, we regain the capacity to choose, rather than merely comply.

Reprogrammed is structured to reveal the hidden mechanisms of modern choice architecture. In the first chapters, we examine the interface itself: how it acts as a mediator, an editor, and ultimately a decision-maker. We look at the invisible choices made in design meetings and encoded into your everyday actions—how friction is removed, how defaults are set, how attention is guided.

From there, we turn to the systems that move us—literally and figuratively. The digital maps we rely on to navigate are not just tools of orientation; they are instruments of automation. They influence not only how we get somewhere, but how we think about distance, efficiency, and value. A route is never just a route—it is a behavioural proposal.

We then dive into the feeds that structure perception. Social platforms and recommendation engines don't just respond to your preferences; they help shape them. What is missing from your feed can be just as consequential as what is present. The algorithms aren't just surfacing content; they're pruning your worldview.

Next, we confront the world of nudging and targeting. Behavioural science meets machine learning in systems that guide not only what we do, but who we become. From personalised ads to frictionless shopping, we examine the subtle but profound ways in which our future selves are being directed, one micro-decision at a time.

As we proceed, the book grapples with a deeper question: What happens to our sense of responsibility, judgement, and identity in a world increasingly mediated by automation? When your calendar suggests your next meeting, your car chooses the lane, and your music app decides your mood, are you still the author of your experience?

We consider not just the tools, but the belief systems they engender. Algorithms acquire an aura of objectivity. Quantified scores come to stand in for quality. Ratings, ranks, and likes begin to substitute for deeper forms of evaluation. What appears neutral is, in fact, deeply normative.

From there, we examine the construction of identity itself—how the self becomes a data product, shaped not only by our own actions, but by the responses we receive, the metrics we internalise, and the personas we curate. In a world where visibility equals value, authenticity becomes a performance.

But this is not a book of despair.

The final chapters offer a map back to agency—not by advocating disconnection, but by encouraging discernment. We make a case for the value of friction: the pause, the prompt, the second guess. True freedom does not lie in effortless execution, but in meaningful reflection. Not every shortcut serves you. Not every suggestion deserves trust.

We highlight designers, activists, and technologists building alternative systems—interfaces that invite choice rather than manage it, protocols that prioritise sovereignty over surveillance, and tools that resist being merely tools of persuasion. The goal is not perfection, but intentionality.

Finally, we leave the reader with a test—a model for knowing when a choice is genuinely yours. We explore how to live consciously within systems you didn't design, and how to futureproof your autonomy as new technologies—ambient computing, generative AI, predictive companions—become even more immersive, and even more persuasive.

A Moment of Reckoning

The promise of the digital age was empowerment. And in many ways, that promise has been fulfilled. But empowerment without awareness is brittle. Convenience without comprehension is a trap.

This book does not ask you to reject technology. It asks you to re-encounter it—with clarity, with scepticism, and with courage. Because the most powerful form of control is the one we do not recognise as such. And the first step toward reclaiming agency is naming the systems that have silently been speaking on our behalf.

The architecture of choice has changed. Let us learn how to live in it—deliberately.

Chapter 1
The Interface is the Intermediary

We seldom recall the interface itself. What lingers in memory is the action—the message sent, the photo shared, the product purchased, the destination reached. Interfaces are designed to vanish in use, to be so seamless and frictionless that their presence barely registers. Yet it is precisely in this vanishing that their influence is most profound. They are not neutral conduits between intention and action; they are meticulously constructed intermediaries, framing our choices, shaping our perceptions, and embedding decisions long before we become conscious of making them.

Take the smartphone home screen. A handful of apps, each with its distinct icon, vie for attention. Their placement is deliberate. Colours, sizes, haptic feedback, even the gesture or biometric used to unlock the device—everything is optimised for speed, circumventing deliberation. You are not selecting from a void; you are choosing from a curated set of possibilities, arranged with intent, often aligned with someone else's priorities rather than your own.

The interface mediates, translates, and shapes. It responds, but also edits. It suggests, defaults, prompts, highlights. Through these mechanisms, convenience becomes a subtle form of control, a choreography of gestures preordained and performed unconsciously. The smoother the interaction, the less visible the intervention, and the greater the influence.

To grasp this, we must discard the notion that interfaces are transparent or passive. They are anything but. Every icon, menu, and constraint reflects deliberate choices by designers, engineers, and product managers, guided by a mesh of usability concerns, engagement metrics, commercial incentives, cultural assumptions, and ethical norms. Far from incidental, these decisions encode priorities into daily life, subtly governing behaviour without overt enforcement.

Consider cookie consent banners. When "Accept All" is presented in bright blue and "Manage Preferences" in muted grey, most users select the former—not out of thoughtful privacy consideration, but because the interface nudges them toward convenience. Choices are subtly funnelled. What appears to be freedom is often guided selection.

This extends beyond pop-ups. Streaming platforms, for instance, craft interfaces to minimise cognitive friction. Autoplay, curated thumbnails, algorithmic rankings—they all conspire to reduce reflection. Users watch, listen, and believe their preferences are honoured, when in truth they are being cultivated. Interactions accumulate over time, shaping not only behaviour but attention, belief, and identity. Interfaces participate in the formation of conduct, scripting behaviour in design languages invisible to most users.

Good design today is judged by invisibility—intuitiveness, effortlessness. Paradoxically, the more invisible the interface, the less we notice its influence. Defaults illustrate this well. Pre-selected options, factory settings, or automated routes exploit status quo bias: people stick with what is given. Altering defaults demands effort, making pre-selection determinative. In organ donation studies, opt-out systems dramatically increase participation compared to opt-in systems, demonstrating that presentation alone can shape outcomes. Interfaces govern not through coercion but through choice architecture.

In the digital world, this logic scales to billions. Navigation apps shape not just individual movement but urban traffic flows. Routes presented as "optimal" carry unseen incentives; alternatives are filtered out. What feels autonomous is, in fact, mediated, wrapped in convenience. The interface answers questions before they are asked.

This is not a dystopian claim, merely an invitation to observe. Every tap, swipe, and scroll is a structured interaction, reflecting upstream design decisions and cascading into downstream behavioural consequences. Interfaces are editors: they highlight, conceal, and prioritise. They embed politics, norms, and assumptions into the everyday. Even language within interfaces—"like," "follow," "share"—codifies behavioural scripts. Acts become gestures, gestures become habits, habits shape belief.

Infinite scroll exemplifies this. Designed to reduce friction, it carries attention forward automatically. The user does not consciously continue scrolling; the interface sustains momentum. Convenience and seamlessness cloak the guidance, making the user complicit in their own redirection.

Yet the interface does not eliminate choice entirely. It structures it—defining the stage, constraining the script, limiting exits. Users retain agency, but within bounds. The risk lies in failing to recognise the framing. Interfaces, after all, are behavioural technologies: micro-decisions at the level of layout, interaction, and navigation cascade into macro-effects on attention, intention, and identity.

From e-commerce to productivity tools, each interface signals priorities, possibilities, and next steps. Behind them lie agendas rarely declared. Recognising this does not demonise design—good interfaces expand access, empower action, and facilitate learning. But unexamined, they can become conduits for passive conformity.

To acknowledge the interface as intermediary is to reclaim the capacity to ask: who made this choice for me, and why? What options remain unseen? What might I do differently if I paused rather than complied? These questions are practical, foundational, and urgent. Digital autonomy begins here: with the tap that feels inevitable, the swipe that feels natural, the screen that seems to anticipate desire before consciousness catches up.

Choice, Wrapped in Convenience

A frictionless experience is rarely neutral. The smoother the interaction, the more invisible the architecture beneath it—yet it is within this very architecture that modern power resides. Interfaces today are not mere conduits between user and function; they are mediators of thought and action. Their design hides layers of complexity, decision-making, and bias under a thin lacquer of ease. What feels intuitive is often engineered. What appears obvious is frequently orchestrated. And what is offered as a "choice" has, more often than not, been pre-sculpted into a predictable shape.

The genius of modern interface design lies in its concealment. Not in hiding features or functionality—though it sometimes does that too—but in hiding influence. When a user unlocks a device, taps a screen, or scrolls through a feed, they are not simply engaging with content or navigating a tool. They are participating in a highly curated experience, one that has been structured to guide, suggest, and often automate decision-making in the name of convenience. We are encouraged to believe we are choosing, when in reality, we are reacting within constraints. It is in this subtle choreography—this wrapping of decision within design—that our autonomy is most quietly reshaped.

Consider the routine act of ordering food through a delivery app. The interface offers categories: "Popular Near You," "Top Picks," "Recommended for You." These labels give the impression of personalised service, of a system that knows your taste. Yet what drives their presentation may be a cocktail of sponsorship deals, algorithmic assumptions, and engagement optimisation strategies. The layout favours certain cuisines, elevates specific vendors, suppresses others. The user experience is smooth, tailored, fast. But what looks like personal preference is in fact a by-product of invisible sorting criteria and platform incentives. The choice is real—but it is narrow, structured, and often misleadingly framed.

This phenomenon is not accidental. It is a product of what the industry hails as good design: minimal cognitive load, reduced steps to action, high conversion rates. These are not inherently malicious metrics, but they are rarely neutral. The language of convenience has become a cover for quiet manipulation, often under the guise of user-centricity. But who defines what's "good" for the user? And to what extent does usability begin to erode deliberation?

Part of the issue lies in the language itself. Words like "seamless," "intuitive," and "frictionless" have become synonymous with progress in interface design. But friction, in many contexts, is not a flaw—it is a cue for reflection. It introduces the pause necessary for evaluation. In contrast, seamlessness flattens decision-making into reflex. The more natural a behaviour feels, the less likely we are to interrogate its source. This is why the most influential interfaces are not those that demand attention, but those that fade into the background, becoming extensions of the hand, the mind, the self.

The deeper effect of such design is the quiet normalisation of passivity. In traditional human decision-making, effort and awareness were often coupled. Choosing a route, selecting a product, or deciding what to read required comparison, trade-off, and intention. Today, digital interfaces assume those burdens. They automate the weighing of alternatives, often before the user is aware an alternative existed. The price for this outsourcing is subtle: a shift in the locus of control, from person to platform.

This transfer is most evident in the use of default settings—pre-configured options that frame user interaction. Defaults do not merely save time; they set norms. They are sticky, persuasive, and powerful. Whether in privacy controls, account preferences, or content filters, users overwhelmingly stick with defaults. Not because these settings reflect deep personal preferences, but because changing them demands awareness, effort, and sometimes specialised knowledge. Defaults work by exploiting inertia—a psychological bias towards maintaining the current state. And because they rarely feel like choices, their consequences often go unnoticed.

A striking example comes from social media platforms, where the default visibility of posts—public, friends-only, or private—can shape not only user behaviour but user identity. A default of public sharing encourages self-presentation, performative curation, and attention-seeking patterns that would not emerge under a more private, deliberative model. Similarly, when platforms default to algorithmic feeds rather than chronological ones, they are making an editorial decision—prioritising what users *should* see, based on metrics like engagement or relevance, rather than letting users determine their own sequence of attention.

At scale, these defaults shape collective behaviour. They determine what becomes popular, what fades into obscurity, and how information circulates. The interface, in this sense, becomes a soft infrastructure of social life—

directing flow without appearing to do so. Its power lies precisely in its plausible deniability.

Yet this orchestration is not confined to social media. Navigation apps present a case study in how interfaces can guide physical movement with profound implications. When Google Maps or Waze recommends the "fastest route," it rarely discloses the criteria used: Is it based solely on traffic? Does it incorporate commercial interests, such as sponsored locations or promoted detours? Does it account for safety, scenic value, or neighbourhood impact? The user, seeing a clean blue line on a screen, simply follows. Trust is given not because the system is transparent, but because it is convenient. The very notion of what it means to choose a path—literally—has been redefined by interface.

This redefinition extends into consumer behaviour. Online retailers design purchase flows that reduce barriers to buying: saved payment methods, one-click checkout, algorithmic recommendations that bundle products together. These affordances accelerate decision-making, but they also bypass deliberation. The line between intention and impulse blurs. When the path from desire to acquisition is frictionless, the threshold for regret lowers. Yet regret, like friction, plays an essential role in regulating behaviour. Without it, consumption becomes automatic, unchecked, and often unconscious.

Some designers defend these dynamics as "helpful nudges"—small interventions that steer users toward beneficial choices. Drawing from behavioural economics, the concept of "choice architecture" has been used to justify design decisions that simplify user experience. But nudging operates on a slippery ethical slope. Who determines what is beneficial? Is a nudge toward healthier eating functionally different from a nudge toward higher ad engagement? In both cases, the user is being steered, not by explicit command but by structural suggestion. And the more these nudges are embedded into the interface, the less visible they become.

This invisibility breeds complacency. When users feel that systems are working "for them," they stop questioning the terms of that service. The rhetoric of personalisation reinforces this dynamic. "Recommended for you" implies that the system understands, adapts, and serves individual preference. But in many cases, what's recommended serves platform objectives—higher watch time, longer sessions, increased monetisation. The interface becomes a salesperson with a disarming smile: always helpful, never impartial.

There is also a deeper philosophical cost to this framing of choice. If every action is guided by a system optimising for convenience, what happens to the practice of autonomy? Autonomy is not merely the ability to choose, but the capacity to reflect on that choice, to wrestle with competing values, to revise and resist. Convenience short-circuits this process. It makes the path of least resistance appear not just easier, but preferable, even virtuous. And in doing so, it erodes the muscle of independent judgement.

That erosion is compounded by a lack of transparency. The logic behind interface decisions—what is shown, what is hidden, what is prompted—is rarely exposed to users. The complexity is abstracted away in the name of elegance. But that abstraction has consequences. When people don't understand the systems shaping their behaviour, they cannot contest them. They cannot ask better questions, because they are not aware questions need asking. The interface becomes not just a guide, but a filter on perception.

Critics may argue that most users do not want complexity—that the average person prefers convenience over control. And there is truth to that. Not everyone wants to tweak every setting, read every privacy policy, or understand every algorithm. But this is a false binary. The choice is not between chaos and coercion, between full autonomy and total automation. It is about *designing with dignity*—creating interfaces that honour the user's capacity for thought without overwhelming them. It is possible to build systems that are both usable and transparent, efficient and respectful.

To do so requires a shift in values. The design culture that celebrates conversion metrics and user retention must make space for ethical reflection. What values are being encoded into the interface? What assumptions about human behaviour are being operationalised? What trade-offs are being made between user benefit and platform gain?

Ultimately, the wrapping of choice in convenience is not a technical inevitability—it is a cultural decision. It reflects what designers, developers, and product leaders believe about their users: Are they agents to be supported, or consumers to be guided? Are they capable of reflection, or do they need shielding from complexity?

The answers to these questions will determine not only the future of interface design, but the shape of human agency in a digital world. For now, we live in a paradox: a world of unprecedented access, wrapped in systems that increasingly pre-arrange our actions. The interface smiles, the options appear, and the decision feels effortless. But the most consequential choices are often the ones we don't know we're making. And the most important form of resistance may begin with a question: Who designed this decision to feel so easy?

Invisible Design, Visible Behaviour

A line of code rarely looks ideological. A font choice does not shout its intent. A colour palette is not immediately political. Yet in the modern world, these quiet decisions made by designers, engineers, and machine systems ripple outward—shaping the routes we take, the stories we believe, the habits we form, and the values we internalise. The most influential forces in contemporary life are no longer delivered through explicit authority or overt persuasion, but through the *subtle scaffolding* of digital environments. The cumulative effect is profound: our behaviours are increasingly not chosen, but *channelled*—directed by systems whose values are embedded not in what they say, but in how they function.

Modern interface design excels at invisibility. This is a feature, not a flaw. The smoother a user's experience, the more the mechanics of that experience dissolve into the background. Good design, in the prevailing view, is the kind that "just works." But when a system "just works," it typically works in ways prefigured by someone else. The very success of interface design—its elegance, speed, and usability—relies on millions of micro-decisions that remain unseen by the end user. And those decisions, often made far upstream, contain within them assumptions about behaviour, desirability, risk, efficiency, and value. The user doesn't see the logic. They *live* its consequences.

Take, for example, the way search engines present information. Users often treat the first few results on Google as objective truth, unaware that placement is shaped by a complex interplay of commercial bidding, algorithmic ranking, and prior user behaviour. The interface itself offers no obvious indication of this sorting mechanism. A search bar, a list of links, perhaps a few labelled ads. But beneath this apparent neutrality lies an engine that, by privileging certain results over others, effectively dictates what counts as relevant, trustworthy, or knowable. The user experiences it as a discovery. In reality, it is a guided reveal.

This subtle shaping extends beyond information retrieval. Consider the layout of a ride-hailing app. When a user opens Uber or Lyft, they see a map with suggested pickup points and estimated times. These are not neutral indicators; they are designed cues meant to guide action. Certain routes are emphasised, certain vehicle types are highlighted, certain pricing options are made prominent. Behind each visual element is a matrix of incentives: reducing driver wait time, increasing throughput, minimising friction. The goal is efficiency, but the effect is behavioural direction. The user *feels* in control. The system has already steered them.

These examples may appear innocuous. But when multiplied across billions of daily interactions, their influence compounds. The decision to emphasise one option over another, to make one action easier than its alternative, becomes not just a design choice but a behavioural intervention. Whether the user is choosing a route, a headline, a product, or a conversation partner, their decision is nested within a framework they did not build and cannot easily interrogate.

The power of invisible design lies in its *pre-emptive logic.* It anticipates behaviour, calculates likely outcomes, and shapes interfaces accordingly. This feedback loop between design and action is reinforced by data. Platforms observe user behaviour at scale, infer patterns, and redesign future experiences to align with those predictions. The result is a kind of anticipatory system: users are increasingly interacting with environments that have already predicted, and subtly nudged, their likely responses. Over time, this reduces behavioural diversity and cements certain usage norms—not because users are forced into them, but because alternatives are never surfaced.

A striking illustration of this dynamic can be seen in the evolution of smart cities. Urban environments are now being infused with data-driven infrastructure—from adaptive traffic lights to surveillance-enabled crowd management. On the surface, these systems promise efficiency, safety, and optimisation. But their design is never value-neutral. A city that prioritises vehicle throughput, for example, may sacrifice walkability and social interaction. A routing algorithm that avoids "high-risk" areas may encode and perpetuate racial or economic biases. These systems shape not just how we move through space, but how we *think* about space—what we deem safe, desirable, or worth preserving.

Design in this context becomes a kind of urban epistemology. It tells us not just where we are, but what the system believes about where we are—and by extension, what it believes about *us*. Behavioural shaping becomes infrastructural. The interface is no longer a screen; it is the built environment itself, digitised and automated.

One might argue that these are unintended consequences—that designers and engineers are simply solving for efficiency or usability, not social transformation. But this is precisely the danger: *intent is not required for influence to occur*. A recommendation algorithm need not intend to radicalise in order to contribute to radicalisation. A predictive policing tool need not intend to profile in order to disproportionately target marginalised communities. The system's logic, once deployed, operates independently of its creators' ideals. The responsibility, therefore, lies not only in design, but in *design awareness*—a recognition that small technical choices can lead to large-scale behavioural shifts.

Compounding this is the increasing reliance on machine learning to make design decisions. When algorithms optimise interface elements in real time—such as button placement, colour schemes, or content order—they are effectively conducting behavioural experiments at scale. The logic here is simple: maximise engagement, retention, or conversion. But the method is opaque. Users do not know they are test subjects. Nor do designers always understand why a given configuration "works" better than another—only that it does. Design becomes a black box. Influence persists, but accountability dissolves.

There is, in all of this, a conceptual tension worth surfacing: the tension between personal agency and system logic. We like to believe that behaviour is a product of will, identity, and context. But when the digital environment is pre-structured by invisible micro-decisions, that belief begins to erode. The user does not see themselves as constrained, but they operate within a space of options that has been *engineered*—often invisibly—to guide, filter, and reward certain actions over others. This is not coercion. It is *calibration*.

To bring this into sharper relief, consider the rise of gamification in behavioural design. Fitness apps, language platforms, and productivity tools increasingly rely on points, streaks, badges, and visual feedback to shape user engagement. These elements, while seemingly trivial, are designed to create *compulsion loops*—structured cycles of behaviour reinforced by reward. Again, the user feels like they are simply participating in a motivating interface. But their actions are being subtly reoriented around system-defined goals. The design does not merely support their intentions; it *restructures* them.

The implications stretch beyond individual psychology into broader epistemic and social domains. When algorithms determine which news stories are promoted, which comments are shown, or which posts receive visibility, they are not just shaping attention—they are shaping *truth-value.* What is seen repeatedly becomes believable. What is omitted becomes irrelevant. The interface becomes an editor, and its design logic becomes a theory of knowledge. This is not an abstract claim. Studies have shown that perceived credibility of information increases with exposure, regardless of factual accuracy. Behavioural visibility becomes a proxy for epistemic authority.

This dynamic is particularly dangerous in polarised information environments. Recommendation systems designed to maximise time-on-platform often cluster users into increasingly narrow ideological funnels. The design logic—engagement—is indifferent to truth, balance, or civic value. What matters is that the user keeps clicking. The result is not just personal bias reinforcement, but collective epistemic fragmentation. Again, the design is not necessarily malicious. But its behaviour-shaping power is real, and often unexamined.

To challenge this requires more than technical fixes. It demands a shift in design philosophy—from one that prioritises behavioural outcomes to one that respects *cognitive integrity.* Users should not be treated as inputs to be shaped, but as *agents* to be supported. This means designing systems that are not merely efficient, but intelligible; not merely persuasive, but dialogical. Transparency, explainability, and user control are not optional ethical add-ons—they are *conditions for responsible influence.*

At its best, design can be empowering. It can support reflection, surface overlooked options, and invite creative expression. But this requires intentionality. It requires acknowledging that every layout, toggle, label, and default carries not just functionality, but *philosophy*. The sooner we recognise that, the better equipped we are to demand—and design—systems that honour rather than hijack human agency.

In the end, what's invisible in design is not absent. It is simply unexamined. But its effects are everywhere, etched into our routines, our decisions, and even our convictions. Behaviour is no longer just a product of will or environment—it is the output of systems quietly scripting our interactions. To see those scripts clearly is not to reject technology, but to reclaim authorship of the choices we make within it.

The Default Effect

Every time you click "Accept" without reading, follow the recommended route without question, or leave a setting unchanged simply because it was already selected, you are engaging with one of the most powerful and underestimated forces in digital life: the default. Defaults shape behaviour not by offering persuasion or argument, but by *disappearing into the background,* quietly leveraging human tendencies towards inertia, trust, and cognitive economy. In environments increasingly defined by speed and overload, the pre-selected becomes the preordained.

Psychologists and behavioural economists have long recognised the potency of default settings in shaping choice. People tend to stick with the option that requires the least effort—physically, cognitively, or socially—to change. This phenomenon, sometimes described as "status quo bias," is not simply laziness. It reflects how the human brain navigates environments of uncertainty and complexity. When the implications of a decision are unclear, when the stakes seem low, or when we assume someone else has optimised the choice for us, we default to the default.

Nowhere is this more consequential than in the design of digital systems, where every interface embeds choices about what is pre-filled, pre-checked, pre-shown, or pre-hidden. The difference between opting in and opting out is not trivial; it is *structural.* And in digital environments, the default is rarely neutral—it reflects a choice made upstream, often by someone with different goals than the end user.

Take privacy settings on major social platforms. When Facebook famously set new accounts to share content publicly by default, the vast majority of users—particularly those unfamiliar with the platform's granular controls—simply left the setting as is. The result was not an intentional public persona, but a default one. Only when public backlash and regulatory scrutiny intensified did the company change the default to "friends only." The lesson was clear: the power to shape user behaviour lies less in the availability of options than in *how those options are presented*—or more precisely, which one is already chosen.

This subtle influence becomes even more significant when the design of defaults intersects with automation. Consider the default route in a navigation app. Google Maps, Apple Maps, and Waze all generate recommended routes based on a combination of speed, historical traffic, and occasionally paid prioritisation. Most users do not investigate alternative paths. The recommendation appears automatically, often highlighted or animated for emphasis, with alternative options greyed out or minimised. Choosing differently requires initiative, confidence, and additional steps. As a result, millions of people follow paths they have not evaluated, through neighbourhoods they do not know, trusting an algorithm's logic more than their own spatial instincts. The behaviour is not irrational. It is efficient. But it is *delegated judgement*, prompted by a default.

The deeper consequence is not just a series of one-off decisions, but a pattern—a shift in how individuals relate to systems. When people repeatedly accept pre-selected options, they begin to internalise a diminished sense of responsibility for those choices. The default becomes a tacit endorsement: *If it wasn't good, why would it be set this way?* This is especially true when the default appears to come from a trusted source, like a familiar brand, a government body, or a widely used platform. The act of questioning the default then becomes not only inconvenient, but socially marked—as unnecessary, even paranoid.

Regulatory frameworks are slowly beginning to acknowledge this dynamic. The European Union's General Data Protection Regulation (GDPR) requires that consent for data collection be "freely given, specific, informed and unambiguous"—a requirement often interpreted to mean that pre-checked boxes cannot constitute valid consent. Yet even with such policies, platforms have found creative ways to maintain behavioural nudges—designing cookie banners that highlight "Accept All" in bright colours while burying granular controls behind multiple clicks. The surface changes, the structure persists.

The psychological mechanics behind the default effect are well-studied. Defaults work by exploiting cognitive heuristics—mental shortcuts that reduce the burden of decision-making. One of the most powerful is *loss aversion*: the tendency to fear losses more than value equivalent gains. Changing a default can feel like incurring a risk, even when the objective outcome is uncertain or minor. Another is the *anchoring effect,* where people's decisions are influenced by the first piece of information they receive—often the default option. Defaults also signal *social norms*. If the system selects a particular choice, it must be the standard, the expectation, the "normal" one. These heuristics are not flaws; they are adaptations. But in engineered environments, they are *exploitable*.

Designers are often aware of this. In behavioural design literature, setting the default is considered a form of "choice architecture"—a way of structuring decisions to produce desired outcomes. Proponents argue that defaults can be used ethically: to promote organ donation, to increase retirement savings, to reduce energy consumption. And indeed, there is evidence that changing defaults in these domains leads to significant behavioural change without limiting freedom. But even well-intentioned defaults raise important ethical questions. Who decides what is "good"? What happens when goals conflict? And how does repeated default-setting affect a person's long-term capacity to make intentional choices?

The issue becomes more urgent when defaults are aligned not with public interest, but with *platform incentives*. Take app permissions on smartphones. Many applications request access to location data, microphone, contacts, and camera—not necessarily to improve functionality, but to collect data for advertising, analytics, or resale. If the default setting grants permission, the majority of users will leave it untouched. If the default denies access and requires users to opt in, permission rates drop dramatically. This isn't just about convenience—it's about asymmetries of information, power, and initiative. The default defines what counts as "normal," and what must be *justified* to change.

This framing—of the default as a cultural and cognitive baseline—helps explain its durability. Once a default becomes normalised, it can persist even when no longer rational. For years, Microsoft Word's default font was Times New Roman 12pt—originally a print standard that migrated into digital text formatting. It became a convention, not because it was optimal for screens, but because it *was already there*. When Microsoft changed the default to Calibri in 2007, there was public debate, even resistance—an indication of how deeply embedded defaults can become in collective habits. The forthcoming change to Aptos as the new standard font is likely to provoke similar discourse, not because of typography, but because of *familiarity*.

In digital product environments, the persistence of defaults can create what might be termed *behavioural path dependence*. Once a user has accepted a pre-set configuration—be it in layout, notification frequency, or algorithmic ranking—the cost of change feels higher with time. Settings are buried in submenus. Language is unclear. Alternatives are untested. The system becomes a closed loop: the user adapts to the default, which reinforces the default's authority. The very friction that defaults avoid on the front end reappears as *resistance to change* on the back end.

Yet there are contexts where defaults are consciously rejected—typically where users feel they have sufficient knowledge, motivation, or stakes. Technologists often tweak operating systems to suit their workflows. Privacy advocates systematically adjust permissions. Power users of financial tools override automation. These examples highlight an important point: *defaults are most powerful where awareness is lowest and stakes seem lowest*. The cumulative effect of many "minor" defaults can be more consequential than a single high-stakes decision, precisely because they fly under the radar of attention.

The design challenge is not to eliminate defaults—no interface can be created without them—but to *make their power visible*. Ethically responsible design means exposing the presence and implications of defaults, making change easy and comprehensible, and acknowledging the behavioural weight they carry. Just as product teams test for usability, they should test for *autonomy load*: How much control does the user retain? How clear is the pathway to alternative choices? Is the default reinforcing a platform's interest or the user's own?

There is a deeper philosophical implication here as well. To be free is not merely to have options, but to *perceive those options as live possibilities*. A menu full of choices means little if one is always pre-selected and the rest are obscure, awkward, or risky to choose. Freedom in digital environments demands *procedural fairness*: not just access to alternatives, but a structure that does not penalise deviation from the norm. The architecture of choice must be navigable, not just present.

Ultimately, the default effect is not a minor quirk of user experience—it is a foundational design principle that shapes how we think, act, and even who we become online. Recognising its influence is the first step toward reclaiming agency. The second is demanding systems that do not conflate ease with endorsement, or convenience with consent. Because what is easy to choose is not always what we *would* choose—if only we were asked, clearly, and with time to consider.

The Interface as Editor

Open any app, search engine, or digital dashboard, and you are not seeing a raw feed of reality—you are seeing *a version* of the world, selected and structured by design. This structuring is not arbitrary. It is editorial. The interface decides what rises to the surface, what is demoted, and what never appears at all. It highlights, buries, omits, and reframes. And like any good editor, it does so under the pretext of clarity, relevance, or utility. But unlike a traditional editor, the interface rarely discloses its criteria.

The notion that user interfaces serve as neutral windows onto data or content is no longer tenable. Every layout, navigation system, menu structure, and feed algorithm is a mechanism of inclusion and exclusion. To design an interface is to decide what counts as visible, what counts as urgent, and what counts as noise. These decisions are rarely explained to users and often unfold invisibly in the background, yet their cumulative influence is substantial. They shape attention, and therefore shape behaviour, belief, and ultimately, worldview.

The clearest manifestation of this editorial function is the algorithmic feed. Social media platforms such as Facebook, Instagram, TikTok, and LinkedIn no longer present content in chronological order. Instead, posts are sorted, filtered, and prioritised by relevance scores, engagement potential, user profiling, and machine-learned predictions. The interface serves not as a passive conduit but as a *dynamic gatekeeper*, curating what the user sees first, most often, or not at all. This affects not only the individual experience but also broader cultural visibility: ideas, people, and perspectives deemed "less engaging" are systematically sidelined.

This mode of editorial control is driven by a mixture of commercial incentives and behavioural science. Platforms compete for attention and design interfaces to optimise for it. The algorithms underlying these interfaces measure what users click, like, share, or linger on, and then amplify similar content to keep them engaged. The result is an environment that rewards high-arousal content—emotionally charged, divisive, entertaining—while sidelining complexity, nuance, or contradiction. The interface, in its pursuit of relevance and retention, distorts salience.

Yet editorial control is not limited to content sorting. It is embedded in visual hierarchy—the size, colour, and placement of buttons; the prominence of headlines versus subtext; the spacing between elements. A brightly coloured "Buy Now" button at the top of a page and a small link to "See More Options" in grey text below are not neutral design choices. They are persuasive tools, steering users towards desired actions. The interface stages a drama in which some actors are given a spotlight and others are relegated to the shadows.

One of the most overlooked domains where interface-as-editor exerts influence is in search. Google's search results page appears as a simple, objective ranking of links, but it is the outcome of a complex system of algorithmic interpretation, advertisement bidding, regional preferences, and historical user behaviour. What appears "at the top" is rarely a measure of truth, but of relevance *as defined by the system*. Most users rarely venture beyond the first page of results. This makes the interface's editorial decisions not only impactful, but near-determinative. If an idea doesn't appear in the first ten results, for many users, it simply doesn't exist.

The same logic applies in productivity and collaboration tools. Platforms like Slack, Microsoft Teams, and Notion guide what information is surfaced, when, and to whom. Notifications, tagging systems, and smart suggestions determine whose voices are heard and whose inputs are delayed or lost. Even time itself is edited: default calendar views emphasise time blocks and meetings, reinforcing a certain mode of work culture—urgent, scheduled, synchronous. Alternative modes—deep work, asynchronous collaboration, reflection—are visually deprioritised.

The editorial logic of interfaces extends into consumer behaviour. E-commerce platforms shape purchasing decisions not only through personalised recommendations, but through subtle choices in sorting and display. What's listed as "Best Value," what's marked as "Most Popular," what reviews are shown first, what filters are applied by default—all of these editorial decisions influence what the user deems trustworthy or desirable. Amazon's interface, for instance, does not merely display products. It frames choices through badges, rankings, and automated comparisons that define how users understand quality and scarcity. The presentation of options alters their perceived legitimacy.

There is also an ethical asymmetry in this editorial function. Traditional media editors are held to normative standards—journalistic ethics, transparency guidelines, editorial accountability. Interfaces, however, operate in an opaque and decentralised way. No single person curates the content, yet the system as a whole performs curatorial functions. The rules governing what gets surfaced are proprietary, constantly shifting, and rarely audited externally. This creates a design epistemology where *power operates without acknowledgement,* and influence masquerades as neutral functionality.

This power is further magnified by personalisation. As interfaces increasingly adapt to individual users—via location data, browsing history, device type, and inferred preferences—the editing becomes bespoke. One person's homepage looks entirely different from another's. The stories shown, the settings offered, the features suggested—all are tailored to optimise user engagement, but in doing so, they narrow the field of experience. This personalisation, while convenient, erodes shared informational ground. It becomes harder to know what others are seeing, or why they are reacting as they are. Interfaces, once seen as gateways to a public digital space, become isolating chambers of editorial echo.

The philosophical implications are substantial. If we accept that every interface is a form of editing, then we must also accept that every interface *frames truth*. Not in the sense of deliberate propaganda, but in the quieter sense of shaping *what counts as available evidence, what is considered worth attention, and what is seen as optional or extraneous*. This editorial framing affects not just what we think about, but what we believe is worth thinking about in the first place.

This editorial role also blurs authorship. In traditional media, we can point to an editor's hand—a byline, an editorial note, a masthead. In interface design, authorship is distributed across UX designers, product managers, behavioural scientists, and algorithms. The decisions are made collaboratively, iteratively, often experimentally. But their outcomes are unified in the interface. The user interacts with a single, coherent editorial reality, even though that reality is the product of fragmented and unaccountable influence.

The challenge is not to eliminate editorial logic from interface design—this would be impossible and undesirable. Any system that offers choices, sorts information, or guides action must apply structure. The real challenge is to make this structure legible, contestable, and humane. Users should not have to reverse-engineer the values behind a platform's editorial choices. Nor should they be forced into engagement paths that serve business metrics at the cost of their own goals. Interfaces must be *interpretable,* not just usable.

There are promising developments in this direction. Some platforms are experimenting with transparent algorithms, allowing users to toggle between personalised and chronological feeds. Others are providing clearer labelling for sponsored content, recommendation engines, or AI-curated summaries. These steps acknowledge the editorial role of design without denying its power. But they remain exceptions. Most interfaces continue to shape experience silently, under the guise of efficiency.

To engage with an interface today is to engage with an *opinionated machine*. It has preferences, biases, habits. It foregrounds some things and backgrounds others. It does not merely respond to your input; it frames your perception of the possible. To see this is not to become cynical, but to become literate. Just as critical readers learn to interrogate how texts are edited, digital citizens must learn to interrogate how interfaces are constructed.

Because in a world increasingly mediated by screens, the shape of our understanding is inextricable from the shape of the interface. What we know is a function of what we see. And what we see is no longer up to us alone. The editor is always present—but now it wears the skin of the interface, and it never signs its name.

Chapter 2
Maps that Move You

There was a time when getting lost was an essential part of moving through the world. To lose one's way was to be present, alert to the subtleties of terrain, light, and signage. It demanded attention, cultivated spatial literacy, and fostered independence. Today, the likelihood of becoming genuinely lost has diminished dramatically. Yet in exchange, something subtler—and perhaps more consequential—has been surrendered: the act of wayfinding itself. It has been outsourced to systems that not only guide movement but shape the imagination of space.

The shift from printed maps to digital navigation represents a profound, yet often overlooked, transformation in modern cognition. Paper maps required interpretation: scale, direction, topography. Routes had to be visualised, landmarks anticipated, choices made along the way. Early GPS systems, though more assistive, still depended on active engagement. Modern mapping interfaces, however, have moved from guide to governor. They no longer merely assist; they decide. Orientation has become automation, and movement itself is increasingly a managed process.

This change is as much behavioural as it is technological. How we navigate informs how we conceive of space, time, and value. The digital map is never neutral; it is a choice-laden interface, engineered to optimise for efficiency, safety, or commercial interest. Routes are calculated continuously, prioritising one path over another, one destination over an alternative. Users rarely question these defaults, and in that trust lies a subtle surrender: the logic of the map becomes the logic of the mover.

Efficiency dominates this logic. When an app suggests the "fastest route," speed is framed as inherently desirable, often without revealing what is sacrificed—scenic value, safety, social encounters, historical context, or local economies. Slow routes become inconveniences; detours, nuisances. Curiosity atrophies. Spatial imagination shrinks. The world becomes a series of algorithmically sanctioned corridors, reducing exploration to optimisation.

This narrowing carries real consequences. Side streets go unnoticed, local cafés unvisited, pedestrian paths ignored. Entire geographies—particularly those lacking rich mapping data—fade from the mental map. Digital navigation channels traffic toward predictable arteries, concentrating activity and reinforcing commercial hierarchies. Behaviour, attention, and even the urban environment itself are subtly redistributed.

Consider the effect of Waze in urban centres. Streets once quiet transform overnight into thoroughfares, rerouted traffic burdening residential areas while affluent zones remain insulated. During the 2020 Black Lives Matter protests in Los Angeles, rerouting to avoid roadblocks shifted congestion into neighbourhoods ill-prepared for it, exposing residents to risk. This was not error; it was optimisation functioning as designed, devoid of context or ethical nuance.

Such outcomes are not malevolent, but they are ideological. They privilege throughput, predictability, and efficiency, rendering other values—serendipity, cultural richness, environmental sensitivity—almost invisible. What is routable becomes legitimate; what is mapped becomes cognitively and commercially real. Computation, by its nature, simplifies. Yet space resists simplification. Cities are layered, living ecosystems of memory, culture, and human behaviour. Routes are not merely about arrival but about passage—who we encounter, what we perceive, how we understand place. When velocity trumps context, experience flattens.

Pedestrian navigation illustrates this further. Turn-by-turn instructions reduce walkers to followers: "turn left, continue 200 metres, your destination is on the right." Curiosity is supplanted by obedience. Journeys once rich in improvisation and discovery become scripted executions. Even the perception of distance shifts. Travel is measured in minutes rather than scale or terrain. Time saved becomes the ultimate metric, subordinating other forms of value—cultural, aesthetic, or environmental.

Agency remains, but it is constrained. Defaults, incentives, and dependence on automation shape habitual deference. The map stops being a suggestion; it becomes a prescription. Exceptions exist—cyclists rerouting for safety, planners scrutinising flows—but the broader pattern persists: navigation interfaces concentrate attention, and through it, reshape urban and social experience. The map influences where people go, which streets thrive, and even which businesses succeed. What began as a tool now operates as a feedback loop: movement justifies the map, and the map shapes movement.

Navigation also encodes moral and socio-political priorities. Choices about which roads to prioritise, which areas to avoid, and which hazards to highlight are informed by data—traffic, accidents, crime—but the data itself carries bias. Systems can inadvertently reproduce inequities, marking certain neighbourhoods as unsafe or inefficient. In this way, the map functions as an actor, mediating not only travel but perception, subtly influencing judgments about people and places.

Resisting this quiet programming begins with awareness. It means recognising that each suggested route is a decision made for you, not by you. It entails occasionally choosing the longer, stranger, or less optimised path. It involves questioning whether efficiency should always take precedence—and what might be gained or preserved when it does not.

The map is not the territory. Yet in contemporary life, the digital map increasingly defines how we navigate the territory. It filters what we see, visit, skip, and value. The benefits—safety, accessibility, real-time insight—are undeniable. Still, the influence of navigation interfaces on perception, behaviour, and spatial imagination demands scrutiny. For when the interface moves you, it also moves your mind. And if we fail to interrogate where it points, we may never notice the roads we have silently abandoned.

From Orientation to Automation

When people once set out on a journey—whether across cities or through unfamiliar neighbourhoods—the act of navigation required a series of conscious, often collaborative, decisions. A printed map would be consulted, oriented by hand, landmarks identified, routes debated. It was not always efficient, but it was attentive. Wayfinding was a skill, rooted in visual cues, local knowledge, and spatial reasoning. Today, this process is collapsing into a single tap on a smartphone screen. Destinations are selected, routes generated, and instructions issued by automated systems that expect obedience more than understanding. What was once a deliberate act of orientation has been transformed into a seamless exercise in automation.

This shift is not merely functional—it is cognitive. Traditional navigation demanded that the traveller internalise the shape of space: where places are in relation to one another, what lies in between, how to get back if lost. You had to *know where you were*, not just physically, but conceptually. Digital navigation, by contrast, replaces spatial knowledge with procedural execution. The user is no longer required to comprehend the environment; only to follow it. Turn left. In 300 metres, take the exit. Recalculating. Direction becomes instruction, and orientation becomes compliance.

The shift from map to app reflects a broader transition in human-tool relations—from analogical aids to algorithmic authority. Paper maps were static, universal, and cognitively demanding. They offered the same information to all users, regardless of their intent or profile. They required interpretation. GPS systems, and especially modern smartphone-based navigation, are dynamic, context-sensitive, and data-driven. They adapt routes in real time based on traffic, time of day, user behaviour, and even third-party commercial incentives. The interface personalises the journey, but also obscures its logic. You are shown *a* route, but not necessarily *why* that route was chosen over others.

That opacity matters. In traditional navigation, every turn chosen carried a rationale: a visual landmark, a remembered shortcut, a street name committed to memory. In digital navigation, the rationale is buried beneath code. You might be rerouted to save thirty seconds, to avoid a construction site, or to serve the traffic flow of the platform's broader user base. You may also be steered based on inputs you didn't knowingly provide—such as location history, user demographics, or commercial partnerships between navigation services and advertisers. The user interface offers clarity. The system behind it withholds complexity.

One of the consequences of this automation is a gradual erosion of what geographers call *cognitive maps*—our internal sense of how places relate to one another. This decline is measurable. Studies have found that individuals who rely heavily on GPS systems show reduced activity in the hippocampus, the region of the brain associated with spatial memory. Put simply, when we no longer need to construct maps in our minds, our ability to do so atrophies. What was once an active engagement with space becomes a passive traversal through it. The world flattens into a series of prompts and arrivals.

This is not simply a matter of neurological concern. It has cultural and behavioural implications. People accustomed to turn-by-turn guidance are less likely to explore spontaneously, less confident in unfamiliar environments, and less capable of rerouting independently when systems fail. They may arrive faster, but they arrive *less informed*. Their relationship with place becomes transactional. This is especially evident in cities, where GPS navigation can lead residents to move through their own neighbourhoods without ever fully learning them—relying on automation even in familiar contexts. The system promises efficiency, and it delivers. But the cost is a narrowing of attention and an outsourcing of judgement.

Consider the architectural analogue: buildings that require wayfinding signage at every junction have not been intuitively designed. Good architecture guides movement through structure, not just instruction. Similarly, environments that are navigable only with digital aid become places we pass through, not places we inhabit. When digital overlays are removed, the environment feels disorienting. This is not a coincidence. It is a dependency engineered through repetition.

There is also a generational divide in how orientation and automation are experienced. Older users, raised with paper maps and memorised routes, often retain a latent awareness of spatial relationships—even when using digital systems. Younger users, for whom GPS has always existed, may lack this comparative frame. For them, movement has always been guided. They are not *becoming* dependent on automation. They were *born* into it. The implications for education, urban design, and emergency preparedness are significant. What happens when a generation raised on automation loses access to its automated systems, even temporarily?

Automation also introduces a paradox: the more the system performs well, the less users are encouraged to understand or question it. Trust increases not through transparency, but through habituation. The system works—until it doesn't. And when it fails, the user is often unprepared. There are documented cases of individuals following GPS instructions into lakes, deserts, or closed roads—not out of irrationality, but out of conditioned obedience. The voice in the interface is persuasive because it is consistent, immediate, and authoritative. The voice in one's head, by contrast, grows quieter.

The more insidious effect is that navigation systems not only guide *how* we move, but *where* we move—thereby influencing economic patterns, social exposure, and political geography. Small businesses may see a dramatic shift in customer flow based on how they are surfaced—or omitted—in mapping apps. Entire districts may experience spikes or drops in traffic due to algorithmic changes invisible to residents. Ride-sharing services rely on navigation apps that direct drivers through routes that privilege speed over social impact. In one widely reported case, navigation apps routed vehicles through residential streets in Los Angeles, turning quiet communities into congested corridors overnight. The system calculated time saved. It did not calculate noise, risk, or neighbourhood integrity.

This raises a deeper question: *whose interests are embedded in the automation of movement?* Navigation services are not public goods. They are commercial products. Their optimisations reflect business logic: reducing server load, increasing user retention, maximising advertising revenue, and avoiding legal liability. These priorities are not necessarily aligned with those of users, cities, or communities. Yet because the interface presents its guidance as neutral—mere instructions based on data—users rarely interrogate its origins. The automation of wayfinding becomes a site of invisible governance.

There are alternatives. Some platforms are experimenting with values-based routing—offering routes that prioritise scenic quality, safety, environmental sustainability, or walkability. Cyclists have long used niche navigation tools that surface routes avoiding high-speed roads. Urban planners are advocating for "legible cities" that support wayfinding without dependence on digital overlays. And some educators are incorporating spatial literacy into curricula—teaching students not just geography, but how to move through space with awareness.

But these efforts remain marginal. The dominant trend is towards deeper automation: real-time congestion analysis, predictive rerouting based on behavioural history, integration with AI-driven assistants that infer destination and purpose before the user inputs it. The future of navigation, it seems, is not just about *getting you there* faster, but about knowing *where you're going* before you do. In such a future, the question of orientation—of where you are in relation to the world—risks being replaced by an answer offered in advance. The system knows. You follow.

Orientation is not just a spatial practice. It is a cognitive one. It is the act of locating oneself in relation to others, to the environment, to intent. When that act is replaced by automation, the experience of space changes. So too does the experience of agency. Automation is not inherently problematic. It reduces friction, increases safety, and enables accessibility. But when it replaces rather than supports human spatial reasoning, it reconfigures not just movement, but meaning.

To navigate is to engage with the world. When systems do it for us, efficiently and invisibly, we risk disengaging from the very spaces we inhabit. The road remains. The arrival occurs. But the relationship to place—once grounded in effort, memory, and curiosity—dissolves into sequence. The map becomes the mover. And we, increasingly, become passengers in our own path.

Shortest Route, Smallest Imagination

Efficiency has become the dominant ethic of modern mobility. Whether commuting to work, running errands, or visiting unfamiliar places, we are now conditioned to expect that digital navigation systems will not only get us there, but get us there *faster*. With a single tap, applications like Google Maps, Waze, and Apple Maps generate the "best" route—best, almost always, by one primary metric: time saved. The result is a seamless experience of movement optimised for speed. But what is lost in this pursuit of efficiency is rarely acknowledged: the richness of spatial experience, the unpredictability of exploration, and the development of a broader geographic sensibility. *The shortest route, as it turns out, often produces the smallest imagination.*

This is not a critique of navigation tools in themselves—they offer clear and legitimate benefits. But there is a cost to allowing algorithms to continually decide where we go and how we get there. The design of these systems encourages obedience to an optimisation logic that prioritises minimal friction over maximal awareness. The user is not encouraged to think about the city as a network of possibilities, but to follow the narrow thread that leads most directly to a destination. Over time, this has profound effects on how we perceive, value, and interact with space.

In traditional wayfinding, getting from one place to another was a creative act. People combined knowledge, experience, and intuition to make decisions. They weighed multiple factors—scenery, safety, congestion, habit, mood. They noticed landmarks, asked for directions, changed their minds. The route was as much part of the experience as the arrival. Now, most of those variables are replaced by a silent, invisible computation. The app calculates and instructs. We follow.

Consider the language of the interface itself. "Fastest route." "Avoid tolls." "ETA: 18 minutes." These are not just factual claims; they are value statements. They encourage the user to see speed and efficiency as primary goods. But why is fastest necessarily best? Could a longer route offer cultural texture, environmental beauty, or personal meaning? These questions are rarely entertained because the design of navigation systems does not make them visible. The algorithm silently suppresses alternative criteria. *What is not counted does not count.*

This tendency is not limited to driving. Walking directions increasingly follow the same optimisation logic. Apps generate routes based on the fewest steps, often without regard for sidewalk quality, lighting, scenic interest, or social vibrancy. Pedestrians are given the fastest path, not necessarily the best one. The city becomes reduced to a transit medium—something to pass through, not engage with. The same holds for cycling apps that prioritise velocity over safety, or public transport maps that omit micro-mobility options altogether.

The broader behavioural effect is a gradual narrowing of spatial attention. Users begin to perceive the world in terms of *what the system shows*, rather than what exists. Streets not included in the recommended path fade into irrelevance. Neighbourhoods not featured in the app's data become invisible. Exploration becomes deviance. Taking a different route requires cognitive effort and goes against the grain of a system that rewards conformity with frictionless performance. And in a digital culture that increasingly prizes ease, friction becomes failure.

This problem is not just individual—it's structural. At scale, the logic of shortest-path routing reshapes urban patterns. Small businesses located off major thoroughfares see reduced traffic because they are not along the algorithm's preferred route. Streets once popular for their ambience or walkability lose visitors because they are no longer surfaced. Tourist flows become concentrated around the most navigated paths, while less accessible cultural assets are neglected. The map creates a feedback loop: the more a route is used, the more it is recommended. The more it is recommended, the more it is used. *Attention follows infrastructure, and infrastructure follows attention.*

There are also demographic and political implications. When routing algorithms prioritise speed, they often divert users away from low-speed zones, pedestrianised areas, or neighbourhoods perceived—rightly or wrongly—as less efficient to traverse. This can contribute to economic marginalisation and reinforce spatial segregation. In cities with historical divides—racial, economic, or infrastructural—navigation systems may quietly entrench existing inequalities. What looks like a neutral calculation is, in fact, a *value-laden redistribution of mobility*.

A 2021 study from the Massachusetts Institute of Technology analysed the long-term effects of navigation apps on urban congestion and neighbourhood equity. It found that while apps reduced average commute times, they increased congestion in previously quiet streets and redistributed traffic in ways that benefited already well-connected zones. The gains were not evenly shared. The system worked—as measured by aggregate speed—but it *worked for whom*?

Some designers and urban theorists have begun to push back against this logic. They argue for a more expansive notion of navigation—one that supports curiosity, engagement, and ethical consideration. The Slow Ways project in the United Kingdom, for instance, offers walking routes between towns and cities based on historical footpaths and scenic trails, not just shortest distance. It is an invitation to reimagine travel as an experience rather than a calculation. Similarly, some experimental apps allow users to prioritise routes with green space, cultural landmarks, or even "most photogenic" views. These tools reintroduce *choice* into a space that had become dominated by algorithmic standardisation.

But these alternatives remain marginal. The dominant platforms still optimise for time and traffic. And because these platforms are used by hundreds of millions of people daily, their design decisions have planetary implications. As we move through the world increasingly guided by algorithms, we begin to *internalise their priorities*. We stop wondering if there is a more interesting way to get somewhere. We stop seeing side streets as invitations. We stop being surprised.

This narrowing of spatial imagination mirrors other forms of cognitive narrowing in the digital age. Just as curated feeds limit our exposure to differing opinions, curated routes limit our exposure to unfamiliar places. The problem is not that we are forced into sameness, but that we *fail to notice* how same our habits have become. What feels like choice is, too often, a preselection. And what feels like convenience is, sometimes, a form of domestication.

This is not an argument against efficiency. Time matters. Convenience has value. But *efficiency should not be the only value embedded in design*. When all routes are optimised for shortest time, we are no longer free to define our own criteria. We are simply accepting the system's defaults. And in doing so, we risk shrinking not just our paths, but our perspective.

A more human-centred approach to navigation would allow users to choose *how* they want to move—not just where they want to go. It would offer filters for experience, not just function: quietest route, greenest path, most historically significant corridor. It would make curiosity as easy as compliance. And it would remind users that space is not something to conquer, but something to *engage with*.

Because ultimately, how we move shapes how we see. And how we see shapes what we imagine is possible. If we want cities that are more inclusive, more sustainable, and more creatively inhabited, we must resist the narrowing influence of systems that reduce space to sequence. The shortest route may save us time. But it may also cost us insight, connection, and a deeper sense of place. And those are losses no algorithm is designed to measure.

Navigation as Behavioural Infrastructure

Cities do not merely organise space; they organise thought. Every road, sidewalk, traffic signal, and transit line communicates an implicit message—not just about how to move, but about *what kind of movement matters*. When combined with digital navigation systems, these infrastructural cues are amplified, reinterpreted, and often re-prioritised in ways that shape not only travel patterns, but habits of perception, expectation, and judgement. *Navigation is not just a means of getting somewhere—it is a system of values, encoded in the built environment and reinforced by the interfaces we use to traverse it.*

This influence begins with a simple premise: *infrastructure is never neutral*. Roads are planned with assumptions about who needs access and who does not. Public transport lines are funded or neglected based on perceived demand, political will, and historical bias. Traffic calming measures appear in some neighbourhoods and not others, reflecting differential notions of safety and risk. The built environment privileges certain routes, speeds, and modes of transport over others. This physical scaffolding trains behaviour—and once that training is absorbed into navigation apps, it gains a second life as digital instruction.

Digital wayfinding systems—whether built into smartphones, vehicles, or wearable devices—do not just reflect the city's infrastructure. They *filter* it. The user never sees the full network of possible paths. Instead, they are offered a few optimised choices, sorted by estimated arrival time, distance, or cost. These filters are not arbitrary. They are behavioural nudges, designed to make certain movements more likely than others. The app's interface becomes a behavioural map: it suggests where to go, how fast, and by what route, reinforcing not only physical flows but cognitive ones.

This co-production of mobility—between physical layout and digital guidance—has far-reaching consequences. It shapes how people perceive speed, safety, and worth, embedding these concepts into everyday routines. For example, when an app consistently recommends driving over walking, it implies that speed is the higher value. When certain areas are labelled "congested," "restricted," or omitted entirely, it signals that they are less desirable or less safe. Over time, users absorb these signals into their own mental maps, *reconfiguring not only how they move, but how they understand the city*.

One of the most pervasive influences is the implicit prioritisation of speed. Navigation systems almost always default to the fastest route, presenting time saved as the clearest measure of value. This logic reflects broader urban planning trends that, for over a century, have privileged vehicular movement over all other forms. Roads were widened, pedestrian spaces narrowed, public transit sidelined—all to facilitate the frictionless flow of cars. Digital navigation systems inherit this legacy. They don't just reflect an existing bias towards speed; they *extend it*, reinforcing it through real-time feedback and dynamic rerouting.

The consequence is not just faster travel, but narrower expectations. Users begin to anticipate constant optimisation. Delays feel like failures, detours like inefficiencies. The city becomes a grid of acceleration, and anything that slows movement—street life, density, interaction—becomes a problem to solve rather than a feature to embrace. This mindset erodes the civic value of slowness, spontaneity, and spatial variation. A well-designed street that invites lingering and social interaction may be algorithmically ignored because it adds two minutes to a journey.

Safety, too, is shaped by this infrastructure-guidance nexus. Navigation systems use data to avoid high-risk areas—accident-prone intersections, crime hotspots, poorly lit streets. On the surface, this seems prudent. But the result is often an uneven distribution of risk and visibility. Neighbourhoods marked as "unsafe" may be routed around so frequently that they become cartographically marginal—less visited, less invested in, less understood. At the same time, areas not flagged may be perceived as universally safe, even if they lack accessibility or inclusivity.

The map edits the city's social reality to fit a behavioural model of avoidance rather than engagement.

These judgements are reinforced by the structure of the interface. A red line on a traffic map evokes urgency. A greyed-out street suggests irrelevance. The hierarchy of information—the colours, icons, route thicknesses—guides user attention and reaction. Rarely are users encouraged to question these representations. The design of the interface hides the assumptions beneath its data. Who decided what counts as safe? Whose mobility counts in calculating "traffic"? What biases are embedded in the accident data or user reports that inform these decisions?

These concerns become more acute when considering *worth*. Navigation systems are not simply technical aids; they are economic instruments. Businesses pay for visibility. Landmarks are curated. Sponsored pins appear on maps not because of their cultural or social importance, but because they have bought a place in the digital landscape. Meanwhile, entire categories of space—informal economies, community gardens, local markets—often remain invisible. The behavioural infrastructure of the app, then, reshapes urban economies, drawing attention and foot traffic towards monetised zones and away from others. *Mobility is not merely optimised; it is commodified.*

The feedback loop is subtle but powerful. As users follow suggested routes, their movements reinforce the platform's assumptions. The system learns that certain paths are popular, certain destinations frequently visited, certain detours rarely taken. This data feeds back into the algorithm, making those same routes even more dominant in future recommendations. Over time, *the behavioural infrastructure begins to overwrite the physical one*, creating new patterns of desirability and neglect not based on planning or need, but on digital repetition.

Urban designers and policy makers are only beginning to grasp the implications of this shift. Traditional infrastructure projects—roads, rail, bridges—are visible, debated, contested. Their impacts can be measured, their priorities scrutinised. But digital behavioural infrastructure is harder to see. It operates in the background, updating constantly, owned and governed by private companies. And yet its effects are profound: *reshaping where people go, how they experience place, and what they come to expect from their cities*.

Some cities have begun experimenting with countermeasures. Paris, for example, has invested in reclaiming streets for pedestrians and cyclists, explicitly challenging the logic of vehicular throughput. Barcelona's "superblocks" redesign urban layouts to reduce traffic and reclaim public space. But even these progressive efforts must now contend with the layer of digital guidance that can undo physical planning. A street closed to through traffic may still appear in navigation apps as a viable route. A new plaza may be ignored because it lacks digital weight. The behavioural infrastructure, unless recalibrated, will resist even the best-designed physical reforms.

There is an urgent need, then, to recognise navigation systems not just as tools of convenience, but as *ideological technologies*. They encode a worldview—about what is valuable, what is safe, what is efficient—and operationalise it at scale. That worldview is not necessarily wrong. But it is partial. It privileges certain forms of movement and marginalises others. It reflects a set of priorities—speed, compliance, monetisation—that may not align with the needs of all users or communities.

To move through a city today is to interact with a dual system: the infrastructure you see and the behavioural infrastructure you follow. The former is made of asphalt and concrete. The latter is made of code and design choices. Both shape your behaviour. Both teach you what matters. And both need to be questioned—because the freedom to move is not just about access. It is about *awareness* of the forces guiding you, and the possibility of resisting or redefining them. The route, after all, is never just a path. It is a proposition. And behind every proposition is a set of values waiting to be uncovered.

When You Don't Choose the Road Taken

In January 2017, during a mass protest against the inauguration of Donald Trump in Washington, D.C., users of the navigation app Waze—unaware of the swelling crowds on the streets—were quietly rerouted through residential neighbourhoods miles from the protest epicentre. The software had fulfilled its algorithmic mandate flawlessly: avoid traffic congestion, reduce estimated arrival time, maximise flow. Yet to the residents of those quiet neighbourhoods, the sudden influx of honking vehicles, irritated drivers, and confused navigation chatter felt like an invisible hand had redirected the pulse of the city into their homes. *The road was not chosen—it was assigned.*

This moment, while seemingly mundane, is emblematic of a deeper shift in the geography of agency. When navigation apps decide routes, the user no longer makes an active choice in the traditional sense. The driver may glance at a screen, accept the "optimised" route, and follow instructions with near-ritualistic compliance. This handover of control feels trivial—what difference could there be between one set of turns and another, so long as the destination is reached? Yet beneath that apparent neutrality lies a profound reorganisation of how decisions are made, whose interests are served, and who bears the burden of algorithmic convenience.

Modern navigation systems do not simply suggest paths; they *allocate traffic.* They perform dynamic routing, adjusting recommendations based on live conditions, historical data, and behavioural modelling. On the surface, this sounds efficient—and often it is. But efficiency for whom? And at what cost? When thousands of drivers are rerouted away from bottlenecks and protests, the result is often a quiet displacement of disruption onto those who never consented to host it. Side streets, once considered local, become arterial. School zones become throughways.

Neighbourhoods designed for walking or quietude are transformed into algorithmic overflow valves. *Traffic does not disappear; it is redistributed, invisibly and without recourse.*

Waze, Google Maps, and other dominant platforms present their routing logic as objective: a mathematical answer to a logistical problem. But every optimisation contains assumptions. Speed is prioritised over serenity. Aggregate outcomes are valued above individual fairness. Consent is not part of the equation. There is no notification to residents that their street will now serve as a high-volume detour for the next six hours. No avenue for objection. In this sense, the algorithm behaves more like an urban planner than a mere tool—but one whose plans are constantly changing, unaccountable, and invisible.

This redistribution is not only physical; it is moral. The costs of inconvenience are offloaded from some onto others. Consider a driver seeking to avoid a traffic jam caused by a street protest—a democratic exercise in public space. When navigation software circumvents the protest, it nullifies one of its primary effects: visible disruption. The protest's signal is weakened, its presence diluted. At scale, the logic of algorithmic avoidance becomes a form of political silencing. *Routing becomes routing around dissent.*

There is a conceptual irony here. These apps were born from an ethos of user empowerment. No longer would we be held hostage by fixed routes, printed maps, or radio traffic updates. With GPS and real-time data, every driver could become a self-optimising node in a network of intelligent mobility. Yet what has emerged is less personal autonomy than *systemic compliance*. Users do not make more choices—they defer more frequently to decisions already made. The default route is selected. Voice guidance is followed. Feedback loops refine predictions, which refine behaviour, which refines predictions. The map learns how you drive and quietly teaches you how to drive like everyone else.

What's left is a narrowing of spatial imagination. The city becomes a hierarchy of algorithmic value. Streets that lead somewhere fast are favoured; those that don't, ignored. The psychological impact is cumulative. When people rely exclusively on apps, they stop remembering routes, discovering places, or developing spatial intuition. They may know how to get from A to B, but have no idea what lies between. The richness of the city—the serendipity of detours, the character of side streets, the encounter with the unexpected—is suppressed in favour of scripted movement. *The urban landscape is no longer explored; it is executed.*

This influence becomes even more ethically fraught when considering *who is affected*. Not all neighbourhoods are equally equipped to handle algorithmic spillover. Wealthier areas often have infrastructural protections—traffic calming measures, speed bumps, residential-only restrictions. Poorer communities may lack such defences, making them more susceptible to rerouted congestion, increased noise, and safety hazards. In Los Angeles, for example, reports emerged of Waze funnelling traffic through working-class areas to avoid freeway bottlenecks—turning side streets into gridlocked corridors and upending the rhythms of daily life. The affected residents had no meaningful recourse. The algorithm had spoken.

Such asymmetries reflect a broader trend: the outsourcing of civic functions to private platforms. Navigation apps are now de facto managers of urban flow. But unlike public transport authorities or city planners, these companies are not accountable to voters, neighbourhood councils, or ethical oversight boards. Their goal is product performance, not equitable mobility. And while they provide remarkable utility, they also displace complexity. The messy, contested business of shared space is reduced to data inputs and output paths. *The city becomes a simulation optimised for frictionlessness, not fairness*.

The consequences are not theoretical. In 2019, an Israeli village sued Waze after it began directing heavy commuter traffic through its narrow streets, disrupting daily life and endangering pedestrians. The company responded that the software was functioning as intended—finding the fastest available routes. In another instance, residents of Leonia, New Jersey, were forced to ban non-local traffic from certain streets after becoming inundated by rerouted vehicles. In both cases, the core issue was not malfunction, but misalignment. The app did what it was designed to do. The problem was *what it was designed to value*.

Reimagining this landscape requires a shift in perspective. Rather than treating navigation apps as neutral utilities, we must understand them as *technologies of influence*. They don't merely reflect our choices—they guide, channel, and constrain them. They operate at the intersection of code, geography, and behaviour, crafting a version of urban reality that privileges certain experiences over others. Recognising this does not require rejecting these tools. It requires interrogating them, demanding transparency, and considering whose interests they serve.

Some technologists are beginning to explore alternative models. Researchers have proposed routing algorithms that consider environmental impact, noise pollution, or social equity—not just speed. Open-source navigation projects invite local communities to define their own priorities. Urban designers advocate for hybrid systems where algorithmic suggestions are balanced by civic goals and democratic oversight. These are early steps, but they point toward a different ethic: one in which *navigation is not simply about getting somewhere fast, but about moving through space in a way that respects context, consequence, and community*.

At stake is more than convenience. As algorithmic systems increasingly govern how we move, they also shape how we relate to place, to each other, and to the idea of agency itself. A road not taken may once have signified a missed opportunity. Today, it may not have been a choice at all. And unless we confront the invisible architecture of algorithmic wayfinding, the road we're on may belong to everyone but us.

Chapter 3
The Feed is the Funnel

Most of us scroll through hundreds of posts each day, each swipe feeling like an act of choice. Yet while feeds appear to offer freedom—a curated banquet of updates, breaking news, niche interests, and memes—they operate more precisely as funnels. Content is not merely presented; it is delivered, carefully structured. And this distinction is far from trivial. We are not simply masters of our informational landscapes; we are participants in systems meticulously designed to capture, shape, and monetise our attention.

The feed is no neutral stream. It is an architecture of influence, constructed not merely to show us what we like but to learn from our behaviour, anticipate engagement, and subtly mould our preferences. What emerges is a space where curation replaces choice, prediction shapes perception, and omission quietly exerts power. Within the rhythmic comfort of personalised content, the underlying logic of modern platforms operates with extraordinary subtlety—and yet, extraordinary effect.

Consider the interface itself. Open Instagram, Facebook, TikTok, or LinkedIn, and content fills the screen without conscious request. The delivery feels effortless. Behind this apparent simplicity, however, lies a vast and opaque machinery. Algorithms absorb signals—what we pause on, skip, click, like, linger over—and feed them into predictive engines that determine the next items presented. Their aim is not simply to inform, but to extend engagement. Preferences are anticipated, gently nudged, even before we realise they exist.

This predictive architecture is where the power of feeds becomes apparent. It blurs the boundary between desire and suggestion. If an algorithm detects interest in climate change content, it may deliver more—but it will also calibrate tone, emphasising whichever narratives maximise attention. Are we drawn to grim forecasts or hopeful innovation? To conflict or consensus? Slowly, subtly, our perception is guided—not maliciously, but mathematically.

The consequences are tangible. Exposure is no longer distributed by editorial judgment, serendipity, or social context; it is optimised for retention and reaction. Attention, rather than accuracy or nuance, becomes the organising principle. Provocation, affirmation, and emotional resonance dominate. Platforms quickly learn that confirmation outperforms contradiction, novelty spikes engagement, and emotionally charged material keeps users scrolling. The result is a feed that magnifies existing worldviews while filtering out counterweights that might temper or broaden them.

This produces what philosophers describe as epistemic closure—not through censorship, but through omission. What never appears on screen is absent from awareness. In an age where feeds serve as primary conduits of news, culture, and political signals, their boundaries effectively define reality. What is missing from the feed becomes missing from the mind.

Interface design reinforces this narrowing. Infinite scroll removes natural stopping points. Metrics of likes and shares act as visible social validation. Recommendation loops lead from one video to the next, from one post to a cluster of similar emotional tones. Curiosity yields to satisficing: we accept the first adequate answer or perspective. Exploration is not punished, but the architecture offers no incentive for it.

Satisficing is by design. Feeds supply just enough novelty to sustain engagement while reducing discomfort. Users are guided through high-probability interactions, subtly conditioned to behave predictably. Habits harden, curiosity contracts, and the algorithm becomes not a mirror but a mould.

The ramifications extend beyond individual cognition. Millions inhabiting personalised funnels generate parallel realities rather than pluralistic discourse. Political debate fractures, cultural consensus diminishes, empathy wanes—not from incapacity, but from reduced exposure to stimuli that would evoke it.

Human editors, once responsible for balance and context, have been replaced by engagement-driven algorithms. Unlike editors, these systems have no commitment to fairness, representation, or epistemic integrity. They optimise for clicks, time on site, and conversions. Falsehoods, conspiracies, or skewed narratives proliferate not out of ideology, but because they perform well. And when such content spreads, it shapes opinions, behaviour, and policy alike.

It is tempting to place responsibility solely on users: diversify your feed, follow new voices, fact-check information. Digital literacy matters, of course—but to leave the burden entirely on individuals ignores the asymmetry of power. Platforms are designed by teams of behavioural scientists and engineers, calibrated for engagement. Users are not on a level playing field. The funnel tilts by design.

Yet agency is not extinguished. Awareness is the first defence. Recognising feeds as products—shaped by commercial incentives, predictive modelling, and frictionless delivery—allows us to interrogate what appears, notice what is absent, and resist automatic scrolling. Some platforms have experimented with chronological feeds, "surprise me" buttons, and features that introduce reflective pauses. These interventions are modest, but they demonstrate that the funnel is not destiny.

Ultimately, the feed is a cognitive infrastructure. Its power lies not in overt manipulation, but in the quiet accumulation of defaults, predictions, and omissions. Understanding this is not paranoia; it is responsibility. In a world rich with information yet poor in attention, what we see is increasingly shaped not by choice, but by what we are shown to choose. Until we trace the contours of that funnel, we remain passengers in a vehicle that always arrives on time—but never asks if the destination was our own.

Curation without Consent

Open your phone and glance at the first few stories that appear on your feed. Pause—not to read, but to ask: who decided that these are the things you should see first? That this tweet, video, update, or headline was more worthy of your attention than the thousands of others published at the same moment? The answer, invariably, is an algorithm. But to call it an algorithm, while technically accurate, dangerously underplays its role. This isn't mere software logic—it's a system of value assignment that structures how you perceive the world. The feed is not simply filtering content; it is *editing your reality*—quietly, persistently, and without asking.

What makes this editing particularly insidious is not that it's hidden in the background—it's that it appears, on the surface, to be entirely neutral. The algorithm is positioned as a technical solution to information overload. Faced with a surplus of digital noise, the feed offers a promise of relevance. It personalises. It adapts. It gets to know you. But this familiarity comes at a cost: *as your feed becomes more "you," it quietly becomes less "them"—less other, less diverse, less surprising*. What begins as convenience ends in constraint.

The modern feed is the culmination of years of refinement in behavioural engineering. Early digital platforms were primarily chronological. Posts appeared in order of publication—what you saw was determined by time, not taste. There was, in that model, an implicit equality of access: every voice entered the timeline on the same terms. But as engagement became the currency of platform growth, chronological order gave way to algorithmic order. And algorithmic order is anything but neutral. It prioritises what is likely to be clicked, liked, shared, and commented on. It learns to favour your past behaviours, reinforce your established preferences, and reward the content styles that keep you scrolling. This is not *curation for clarity*—this is *curation for capture.*

The line between personalisation and manipulation is thin, and increasingly blurred. Consider a platform like YouTube. Watch a video on climate change scepticism, and the recommended queue quickly fills with adjacent videos that often double down on that scepticism. Watch a video on racial justice, and the system surfaces content steeped in activism or—just as easily—reactionary critique, depending on which thumbnails you've hovered over in the past. The system is not ideological; it is opportunistic. Its only consistent loyalty is to engagement. *The most provocative, polarising, or emotionally intense content outperforms the merely informative every time.* The algorithm learns this quickly—and so does the user, often unconsciously.

This is where the issue of consent becomes most acute. Most users are not aware of how their feeds are shaped. They do not opt into algorithmic sorting in any meaningful sense. The mechanics are buried in abstruse terms of service, toggled by obscure settings, or framed as optional features that come pre-enabled by default. More troubling still, even when users understand that algorithms are at work, they rarely grasp the depth of their influence. They think they are seeing "the best" or "most relevant" content—when in fact, they are seeing the *most engaging for them, based on a statistical model optimised for time-on-platform*. It is *personalised relevance as proxy for truth*—a subtle shift that rewires epistemic habits.

The narrowing effect is cumulative. Over time, the algorithm builds a behavioural portrait: your likes, your pauses, your swipes, your click-throughs, your bounce rate. This data feeds a model that predicts what content will keep you active. The model then curates the feed to match. What emerges is a feedback loop: *the more the system gives you what it thinks you want, the more you become the kind of user the system expects*. Divergence is disincentivised. Curiosity becomes bounded by design. Platforms learn to feed your desires before you're aware you have them—and to prevent the surfacing of content that might disrupt your patterns.

This leads to what media theorists call *filter bubbles*—epistemic environments in which one's worldview is reinforced by selective exposure to information. But the metaphor is imperfect. Bubbles suggest fragility and transparency. Algorithmic feeds are more like silos: opaque, layered, fortified by code. The content not shown becomes the most powerful editorial choice. You cannot challenge what you never encounter. This makes omission a form of influence that is harder to detect than bias. *The most significant editorial act is not choosing what to feature—it is deciding what to leave out entirely.*

The implications of this silent narrowing are profound. In democracies, informed citizens are the cornerstone of civic life. But when citizens receive information filtered through opaque engagement-maximising systems, public discourse fragments. People no longer merely disagree—they inhabit informational universes that rarely overlap. Debate turns into dismissal. Dialogue is replaced by disbelief. The curation is not overtly partisan, but the result is often more extreme than traditional editorial bias: *it is micro-targeted cognitive shaping, scaled to billions of users*.

Critically, this system evolves with us. As people change, so do their feeds. But the direction of change is not always self-determined. Algorithms nudge rather than dictate—but persistent nudging creates habits, and habits create identities. A teenager exploring feminism may be routed toward performative activism or, conversely, toward anti-feminist backlash, depending on how the system interprets her earliest clicks. An older man watching videos about financial independence may find his feed slipping into libertarian economics or conspiratorial thinking. The path is shaped not by a search for truth, but by a model optimised for engagement velocity.

It's easy to believe that intelligent people can outthink the feed—that professionals, researchers, and thoughtful students are immune to such influence. But *intelligence does not immunise against manipulation when the manipulation is embedded in the interface*. The most educated minds are often the busiest. When time is scarce, users default to what is served. Trust in the platform's authority replaces critical discernment. The cost of filtering is outsourced to the system, and *the user begins to consume not what is true, but what is algorithmically convenient*.

What would consent look like in this context? Not a passive agreement buried in legal jargon, but an active engagement with how one's informational environment is structured. It would mean transparent algorithms, adjustable feed logic, clear controls over recommendation mechanisms, and a right to know why something appeared—or failed to appear—in one's timeline. It would mean restoring some measure of agency over the vectors of attention.

Some platforms have started to offer chronological timelines or alternative sorting modes, but these are often buried in secondary menus, designed to be forgotten. Others provide "why you're seeing this post" notices, but these are superficial—pointing to vague behavioural signals rather than the underlying logic of optimisation. The most promising efforts come from open-source or decentralised platforms experimenting with user-tuned algorithms—allowing individuals to select the principles by which their feeds are shaped: diversity, novelty, contradiction, civic relevance. But such tools remain marginal, dwarfed by the scale of mainstream systems.

There is no simple solution to algorithmic curation. The volume of digital content is too vast for manual filtering. But what's needed is not a return to pre-algorithmic innocence—it is *a deliberate, transparent, and ethical recalibration of how feeds are constructed.* This requires confronting the business models that underpin them. As long as attention equals revenue, the system will privilege engagement over enlightenment. The real challenge is structural: *to build platforms that treat attention not as a commodity, but as a civic resource.*

Until that shift occurs, users must navigate their feeds with suspicion, curiosity, and care. Not paranoia—but *practical epistemic vigilance*. Ask what's missing. Follow accounts you disagree with. Exit the feed occasionally and enter spaces designed for reflection, not reaction. Every small act of curation reclaims a measure of consent.

Because the truth is simple but stark: if you are not curating your feed, someone—or something—else is doing it for you. And what you see shapes what you know, what you believe, and ultimately, who you become.

Prediction Becomes Prescription

When a streaming service recommends a film, a retailer surfaces a product, or a social feed queues up another short-form video, the logic underpinning each suggestion is neither neutral nor merely responsive. These are not passive reflections of what we might like—they are pre-emptive decisions about what we will see, engage with, and believe next. Predictive analytics, once framed as tools to understand human behaviour, have matured into instruments that quietly shape it. *What begins as probability becomes guidance, and what feels like personalisation becomes prescription.*

The original promise of predictive systems was seductive in its simplicity: by analysing past choices, technology could anticipate our future needs. This was especially compelling in information-rich environments where the friction of decision-making was high. In theory, intelligent filtering should have alleviated cognitive overload. Yet the real power of predictive analytics is not in removing friction, but in scripting it—curating the very conditions in which users operate, deciding what options surface, and subtly steering choices before conscious deliberation begins.

This shift from prediction to prescription is not incidental. It aligns with a deeper economic logic within platform capitalism. Recommendation engines—whether in e-commerce, entertainment, news, or social media—are not designed merely to reflect user taste; they are optimised to drive platform-specific objectives: time-on-site, click-through rates, ad impressions, conversions. *The algorithm is not serving you—it is serving its own utility function, one which often treats user attention as a means, not an end.* Over time, the outputs of these systems do more than accommodate preferences; they shape them, recondition them, and, increasingly, determine them.

Nowhere is this more apparent than in the architecture of content feeds. On platforms like TikTok, YouTube, or Instagram, the feed is not a canvas of choice but a funnel of influence. Engagement metrics become the de facto proxies for relevance, and the content you are likely to watch again becomes the content you are most consistently shown. If you dwell momentarily on a video about urban gardening, you may find your feed rapidly colonised by plant influencers, vertical farms, and compost hacks—not because you decided this was your new passion, but because the system interpreted a moment's pause as preference. The algorithmic inference becomes a behavioural script.

This phenomenon is sometimes described as the "looping effect" of machine learning systems: *human behaviour trains the system, which in turn trains human behaviour, in a recursive feedback cycle that narrows over time.* In this loop, novelty is penalised, surprise is minimised, and divergence from established behavioural patterns is algorithmically discouraged. Over time, the feed becomes a hall of mirrors—not showing you the world, but reflecting back a refined image of what you've already indicated you're inclined to see. This doesn't merely predict your interests; it prescribes your identity.

Consider the implications for political opinion. In 2017, researchers at Stanford University and the University of Chicago found that exposure to opposing viewpoints on social media often made users more entrenched in their existing beliefs, not less. Platforms designed to recommend more of what keeps users engaged systematically avoid surfacing content that might challenge them. Controversy may be monetisable, but contradiction is often not. The result is not just ideological siloing, but the quiet suppression of epistemic risk—the kind of friction that is essential to robust thinking and democratic discourse.

A similar pattern can be observed in commerce. When Amazon predicts that you'll want a particular brand of batteries or headphones, it subtly restructures the commercial landscape. Sellers are incentivised to optimise for visibility within the algorithm rather than quality or innovation. This has produced what some scholars term "algorithmic monocultures"—marketplaces dominated by sameness, where products converge in appearance, description, and user ratings because variation can cost visibility. The consumer, believing they are making informed choices, is in fact choosing from a constrained set preordained by a logic they cannot see.

What makes these dynamics especially challenging is their opacity. Predictive algorithms are rarely intelligible to the end user, and often not even to the developers who build them. Deep learning systems operate as black boxes—highly efficient, poorly explainable. Their outputs appear neutral, automated, and even objective. But the data that trains them is embedded with social patterns, historical bias, and cultural context. A system trained on what people "liked" in the past may entrench existing stereotypes or inequities, all while appearing apolitical.

In education technology, for instance, platforms that recommend courses or career paths based on student interaction data can unintentionally reinforce social stratification. A student from a low-income background who searches for vocational training might be steered toward a narrower range of options than their more affluent peers—not because of aptitude, but because the system presumes a trajectory based on prior users "like them." This is not mere responsiveness; it is path-dependence, engineered at scale.

Even in matters of health, predictive analytics have begun to steer behaviour. Fitness apps recommend routines, eating patterns, or meditation tracks based not just on your history, but on your predicted engagement. This can be helpful, but it also introduces subtle coercion. When "recommended for you" becomes a badge of authority, users often defer to the suggestion rather than deliberate actively. The machine's output begins to carry epistemic weight. *To be predicted is to be profiled; to be profiled is to be guided; and to be guided—repeatedly—is to be changed.*

This raises an ethical imperative: at what point does optimisation become manipulation? When does efficiency in choice become erosion of autonomy? If predictive systems succeed in capturing our attention, redirecting our behaviour, and reshaping our preferences, what room is left for reflective agency? These are not abstract questions. They go to the heart of what it means to choose, to learn, to develop desires not pre-authored by systems trained to anticipate and monetise them.

Some developers argue that personalisation is a form of care—a way of tailoring digital environments to individual needs. And in some cases, it is. But care without consent becomes control. The assumption that the best choice is the one predicted most accurately reduces the individual to a data point, a statistical output. It neglects the non-linear, improvisational, and occasionally irrational nature of human growth. We do not always want what we've wanted before. We do not always benefit from what suits our patterns. *To be human is to surprise oneself.*

A more defensible model of prediction would involve intelligibility, consent, and friction. Users could be shown why a recommendation is being made, offered counter-suggestions, or allowed to modify the criteria by which predictions are generated. Rather than presenting prediction as destiny, platforms could frame it as a hypothesis—one subject to scrutiny, error, and choice. But this requires a conceptual shift: from predictive systems as puppeteers to predictive systems as interlocutors.

As long as the interface hides its assumptions, the predictions it produces will shape users invisibly, irresistibly, and often unknowingly. When the logic of guidance is opaque and the freedom to deviate is functionally absent, prescription masquerades as convenience. The feed, the suggestion box, the autoplay carousel—these are no longer tools for exploration; they are frameworks for behaviour.

Understanding this transformation is vital not to reject predictive analytics outright, but to reclaim agency within them. *The future is not written by the algorithm—but it is being drafted, line by line, in its suggestions. The question is whether we are co-authoring that future—or simply signing our names beneath a script we never saw being written.*

What's Missing from Your Feed?

If the feed is your window to the world, then the algorithm is the curtain—deciding not only what to reveal, but what to conceal. Most users experience digital content as a stream of things shown. But equally—often more crucially—it is a stream of things *not* shown. Feeds, timelines, recommendation systems, and search results present themselves as passive reflections of our interests. In practice, they are carefully engineered to exclude. *What is omitted is not random; it is strategic.* And over time, it cultivates a blindness that feels like clarity.

The modern information diet is curated not just by personal choice but by opaque optimisation functions built to maximise engagement. These systems prioritise salience, emotionality, and click-through potential—not epistemic diversity or contextual balance. When engagement becomes the objective, omission becomes the tactic. The less provocative, the slower to reward, the more complex or demanding—these fall quietly off the table. This produces what could be called an "attention extractive" model of knowledge: the value of content is judged by its capacity to capture, not its capacity to inform.

That distinction matters. In older models of editorial mediation—newspapers, public broadcasting, academic publishing—content selection was guided (at least aspirationally) by relevance, rigour, and public interest. Today, the gatekeeper is a statistical engine that optimises for behavioural response. This shift moves us from *editorial logic* to *algorithmic logic*. It does not merely decide what rises to the top; it filters what never enters at all. The result is a personal feed that appears to reflect your world—but in truth, limits it to a narrow, data-shaped shadow.

Take, for example, the experience of two users searching for the same term—say, "climate change." On Google, one might receive a slate of mainstream scientific consensus; another might encounter hyper-partisan articles, policy scepticism, or YouTube thumbnails with high-contrast fonts and doom-laden commentary. This divergence is not based on user intent, but on prior behaviour—click history, location, device model, inferred interests. Over time, these differences compound. The user is not simply *shown* different content—they are *trained* into different mental models. *The invisible absence of what might have been seen becomes a form of cognitive infrastructure.*

This filtering is most potent where curiosity is passive. Scrolling through a feed is not an act of active inquiry; it is ambient exposure. The stories that appear are not chosen, they arrive. And the stories that never appear are not rejected—they are never imagined. This is what makes epistemic omission so structurally dangerous: the user does not sense what is missing. There is no redacted line, no placeholder, no gap in the scroll. It is not censorship in the traditional sense; it is subtraction by design.

We see this most starkly during times of political tension or global crisis. During the 2021 conflict in Gaza, studies revealed that users of different social platforms encountered radically different versions of events—not because of overt censorship, but because of algorithmic priorities. Stories with emotionally charged imagery, tribal affirmation, or "rage clicks" surged, while nuanced reporting, longer-form explainer content, or historical context languished. This isn't merely a skew in tone—it's a skew in *world-building*. Over time, the omission of certain facts, framings, or perspectives leads to users inhabiting informational microclimates where only particular narratives can flourish.

This phenomenon has roots in older media structures but is vastly amplified by today's platform architecture. Unlike television, which offered a limited number of channels, algorithmic feeds offer the illusion of infinite choice. Yet that very infinity masks an invisible narrowing: *the more a system learns about what you'll engage with, the less it bothers showing you anything else.* This creates a paradox. The more personalised the experience, the less expansive the worldview. The user may feel perfectly informed while being structurally misinformed—not through exposure to falsehood, but through the erosion of contrast.

There is an intellectual cost to this. Curiosity, critical thinking, and epistemic humility require exposure to difference—not only of opinion, but of framing, method, and sensibility. When a feed removes the friction of encounter—when it spares the user from complexity, contradiction, or slowness—it also deprives them of the very conditions that produce depth. *What's missing from your feed is often what's missing from your reasoning: the unfamiliar, the slow-burning, the difficult to categorise.*

This is not a call for nostalgic return to gatekept media; many of those systems had their own exclusions, often driven by ideology or market pressure. But it is a call to recognise that algorithmic omission is not neutral. When recommendation engines suppress indigenous reporting, minority perspectives, non-English sources, or slower investigative formats, they do not just reduce diversity—they create a world in which those voices appear not to exist. *The epistemic cost of omission is not just ignorance; it is disconnection from shared reality.*

This problem is compounded by the absence of transparency. Most platforms do not disclose what has been excluded from your feed—or why. There is no audit trail of suppressed stories, no menu of what might have been shown. The algorithm's logic is treated as proprietary. The result is a population of users who navigate the world through windows whose size, shape, and tint are constantly shifting, but whose frames are invisible.

Even platforms that offer some user control—say, by allowing you to follow specific accounts—often override these preferences in favour of algorithmic curation. Instagram's Explore tab, Twitter's For You timeline, Facebook's Suggested Posts—these are not passive add-ons; they are engineered interventions. They insert "what you might like" above "what you asked to see." And what you might like is inferred not just from your explicit behaviour, but from a computational guess about what will extend your session.

There is a growing recognition of this problem within academic and journalistic circles. The concept of "epistemic injustice"—first articulated by philosopher Miranda

Fricker—speaks to the structural marginalisation of certain voices and perspectives in processes of knowledge production. In the context of algorithmic feeds, this injustice takes the form of *algorithmic silence*: certain communities are not just underrepresented; they are unrepresented, absent not due to merit, but due to model optimisation.

Consider a teenager whose TikTok feed is saturated with beauty tips, fashion trends, and influencer skits. Without deliberate effort or interruption, they may never encounter content about civic participation, science, or global affairs. This is not because the content does not exist, but because the system has decided it is unlikely to perform. The user's world is narrowed not by what they reject, but by what they are never offered. *The unseen is not evaluated—it is simply absent.*

What's at stake here is not just a better recommendation engine, but a deeper question: *How do we preserve informational plurality in a system optimised for attention?* How do we build digital infrastructures that surface not only what confirms, but what challenges? Not only what engages, but what informs?

One promising approach is friction. By designing feeds that occasionally interrupt the loop—introducing randomised content, dissenting views, or contextually relevant alternatives—platforms can create small moments of epistemic expansion. Another approach is auditability: giving users tools to see what types of content they *don't* encounter, and why. A "blind spot index," for instance, could highlight areas systematically absent from a user's consumption pattern, not to shame, but to reveal.

Ultimately, the answer may not lie in the algorithm alone, but in a broader cultural revaluation of curiosity over convenience. Platforms are not solely to blame; they reflect and amplify human tendencies. But they also shape them. By rendering the invisible visible—by making omission something we can see, question, and adjust—we can begin to reclaim not only our feeds, but our attention, our agency, and our capacity to think beyond the edges of what has already been shown.

Scroll to Satisfice

A thumb flick and the screen reloads. Another flick, and a new set of headlines, memes, and product suggestions materialise—none requested, all selected. Infinite scroll is not merely a design feature; it is a behavioural infrastructure. It simulates abundance while eroding intention, flooding the mind with content without requiring deliberation. By removing friction and endpoint, it invites passive engagement—where stopping feels more like abandonment than choice. The result is not enhanced freedom but a continuous narrowing of attention. *Satisfice*—to settle for the minimally acceptable—was once a compromise under pressure. Online, it has become a default mode of cognition, baked into interface logic and driven by engagement incentives.

The infinite scroll was not invented to dull minds but to retain them. First deployed by Aza Raskin in 2006 as a clever UX solution, it has since been weaponised by attention-driven business models. Platforms like Facebook, TikTok, YouTube, and Instagram now rely on endless content flows to generate advertising impressions, harvest behavioural data, and extract attention metrics. Yet while these platforms profit from the scroll's inertia, users pay in cognitive cost. The design converts intention into impulse. When choice is always available yet never required, exploration gives way to repetition.

Engagement becomes the interface's highest currency—not insight, reflection, or informed thought. Each interaction is reduced to a quantifiable response: like, view, share, repeat. The architecture discourages depth and rewards immediacy. A headline is more likely to be engaged with than the article beneath it. A thumbnail more than the video it fronts. And a hot take more than its retraction. This pattern creates an environment optimised not for understanding, but for behavioural frictionlessness—where attention follows the path of least resistance.

This is not an incidental flaw. It is the point. Attention, once treated as a faculty of agency, is now a programmable variable. When combined with algorithmic curation, infinite scroll becomes an instrument of *behavioural conditioning*. Each flick is a lever pull in a digital Skinner box. Likes and views function as variable rewards—highly addictive, statistically unpredictable, and neurologically reinforcing. This is the architecture of compulsion. But it masquerades as convenience.

The epistemological implications are profound. Content exposure becomes a function of feedback loops rather than breadth of curiosity. Once a user begins engaging with a specific type of content—say, videos mocking a political figure or posts about a niche conspiracy—future recommendations skew increasingly in that direction. The feed does not question preference; it exaggerates it. This process, rooted in predictive algorithms and engagement metrics, turns curiosity into conformity. *The more you like, the less you look.*

This narrowing is not just a personal matter—it has collective consequences. As people spend more time scrolling and less time selecting, the ecosystem of ideas shrinks. Marginal viewpoints, emerging issues, and dissenting perspectives are algorithmically filtered out—not by suppression, but by omission. They are not flagged or banned; they simply fail to perform. And what fails to perform disappears. *Epistemic blind spots are not created by censorship, but by engagement asymmetries.*

Consider the information architecture of a typical social feed. Posts that provoke outrage or humour outperform those that require nuance. Clickbait headlines, misleading thumbnails, and sensational claims receive algorithmic amplification—not because they are true, but because they provoke interaction. *Truth competes with virality, and often loses.* Even when a user tries to break the pattern, the design resists. Unlike books, where turning a page is intentional and sequential, infinite scroll erases boundaries between content types. A climate report is sandwiched between a dance video and an ad for supplements. The hierarchy of information collapses into a sequence of impressions.

Even the act of pausing has been redefined. To stop scrolling is to exit the platform. There is no natural endpoint, no "last page" or "you're all caught up." This structural absence trains users to keep going—not because the next post is vital, but because the end never comes. This has a psychological corollary: *completion becomes impossible; satisfaction becomes irrelevant*. And with no signal to conclude, users surrender to perpetual scanning.

This interface logic not only affects what users consume, but how they evaluate it. Fast scroll speeds reduce the likelihood of critical reflection. The brain processes headlines faster than it can assess their validity. Visual repetition induces familiarity, which research shows can increase perceived truthfulness—a phenomenon known as the "illusory truth effect." As such, falsehoods are not debated, they are echoed. Belief reinforcement occurs not through argument, but through exposure. And exposure is algorithmically curated based on past behaviour.

None of this was inevitable. Interface design always reflects values—often unspoken, sometimes unexamined. The infinite scroll could have included meaningful friction points: bookmarks, reflection prompts, time caps, or reading summaries. Platforms could have prioritised content diversity over click-through rates. Algorithms could have been optimised for novelty, contradiction, or thought-provocation rather than homogeneity and volume. But those design choices would have served cognition rather than revenue.

It is tempting to cast the user as passive in this exchange—as if mindless scrolling were an affliction imposed from above. But that would obscure the symbiosis at play. *Users scroll because it is easy; platforms build for ease because it pays.* The real casualty is not free will, but deliberate will. Cognitive laziness is not enforced; it is incentivised. And when frictionless interaction becomes a universal standard, *the act of choosing itself begins to feel like work.*

Yet the harm is not only cognitive—it is civic. Democracies depend on informed citizens capable of grappling with complexity. Infinite scroll undermines that capacity. It flattens public discourse, hollows out attention spans, and conditions users to consume rather than question. When people satisfice their beliefs—gravitating toward plausible-enough explanations or emotionally satisfying claims—they become more susceptible to manipulation, polarisation, and ideological drift. This is not a matter of digital hygiene; it is a question of civic resilience.

Some platforms are beginning to reckon with these effects. Instagram's "You're All Caught Up" prompt was one early attempt to reintroduce a stopping cue. Twitter (now X) has experimented with prompts to read an article before retweeting. YouTube has added break reminders. But these are cosmetic, not structural, interventions. The core incentives remain unchanged: more time on site equals more revenue. And as long as that calculus governs design, the scroll will always favour velocity over veracity.

The challenge, then, is not only technical but cultural. Designers must ask not just *can* we keep users engaged, but *should* we? Users must ask not what content is available, but what is missing. And societies must confront whether a platform's convenience justifies its consequences. Because in the age of the infinite scroll, the question is no longer what we find—but what we fail to notice, because we were too busy flicking past it. *To satisfice is not to decide—it is to defer. And in deferring, we become shaped by what we did not choose.*

Chapter 4
Nudged into Now

You did not select the advertisement that appeared in your feed, nor the headline that followed it, nor the product suggestion that surfaced in a different app minutes later. Yet the system knows why you encountered them. Not because it has intimate knowledge of you, but because it has tracked, compared, and clustered your behaviour—scored it, cross-referenced it, placed you into thousands of overlapping demographic, psychological, and behavioural microsegments. The result is a digital ecosystem not simply responsive to your preferences but anticipatory, interventionist, and self-reinforcing. The shift is subtle: it is not merely that we are nudged, but that we inhabit the infrastructure that nudges.

Persuasion today no longer needs to shout. It whispers. The crude pop-ups and banner ads of old have been replaced by predictive recommendations, frictionless interfaces, emotionally calibrated prompts, and timely notifications. Coercion is unnecessary; the system removes the need for deliberation entirely. What appears as self-direction is often a carefully orchestrated path, engineered partly by your own past behaviour.

At the heart of this lies behavioural targeting—not simply categorising people, but learning how they act in real time. What hour do you click most? Which messages spark curiosity? How long do you pause before scrolling? Every micro-interaction becomes data in a feedback loop that updates constantly, shaping not just what you prefer, but who you are becoming. Prediction turns into participation, and participation into programming.

The consequences extend far beyond shoe advertisements. The same architecture informs voting behaviour, health choices, financial decisions, emotional vulnerabilities, and cultural alignments. Microtargeting does not merely sell products; it shapes political discourse, influences compliance with health directives, and reinforces ideological silos. And because it operates beneath conscious awareness, its effects are rarely recognised, let alone scrutinised. What is at stake is not only attention but orientation—the scaffolding through which we navigate reality.

The efficiency of these systems is often praised as personalisation. But personalisation is not neutral. It is a feedback loop privileging continuity over complexity, past patterns over potential, the familiar over the strange. The playlist suggesting "more like this," the news feed highlighting content aligned with your views, the app prompting your habitual choice—each is a form of computational comfort, reducing novelty in favour of predictability. Over time, deviation becomes effortful; systems are designed to minimise it.

This removal of friction is celebrated as progress, but friction has cognitive value. It allows evaluation, hesitation, reflection. Optimising for immediacy shortens—or eliminates—the moments in which one might pause: Do I need this? Is this source reliable? Do I really want to watch another episode? Speed is mistaken for freedom, yet the result is acceleration—life hurried along by systems that equate ease with agency.

As choice architecture becomes embedded across platforms, apps, and environments, it evolves from persuasion into infrastructure. What was once optional design now becomes invisible default. Checkout flows nudge towards auto-renewal. Health apps suggest goals determined by the system. Dating platforms order profiles to maximise swipes rather than long-term compatibility. These are not random conveniences but deliberate constraints shaping thought, feeling, and behaviour—not only as consumers, but as citizens, parents, partners, and workers.

This is not dystopian fantasy; it is daily life in digitally mediated societies. Influence no longer persuades; it precedes choice. The system ensures you encounter only what makes a particular course of action feel natural. And the more natural it feels, the less it is questioned.

The concern is not simply moral; it is infrastructural. Systems that guide behaviour quietly accumulate power. A thousand subtle nudges over time shape identity as surely as a single major decision might. Repeated suggestion, prioritisation, and convenience produce path dependencies: some futures are more likely simply because they were more accessible in the past.

These mechanisms also reshape self-perception. When choices are always confirmed, preferences reflected, biases unchallenged, reinforcement is mistaken for reality. And when that reinforcement aligns with platform goals, the system does not merely reflect who you are—it teaches you who to become.

This presents a profound tension for societies that prize autonomy, pluralism, and democratic engagement. If freedom is experienced as ease, and ease is shaped by commercial and computational priorities, freedom risks being indistinguishable from conformity. The promise of the digital age—abundant access, diverse voices, boundless possibility—becomes filtered, structured, and rendered invisible, shaping not only what is chosen but how choice itself appears.

The following chapter explores this transformation, from the microtargeted nudge to the infrastructural logic behind it. It invites readers to examine not only what influences their choices, but how influence is embedded in everyday interactions. It interrogates the cost of living within systems designed to reduce friction while also reducing reflection, and it considers what it means to reclaim agency—not by rejecting influence outright, but by recognising its mechanisms, challenging its assumptions, and restoring deliberation in a world designed to remove it. The question is no longer whether we are being nudged, but whether we even notice that we are.

Microtargeting, Macro Effects

A product ad that knows your insecurities. A political message tailored to your demographic fears. A dating suggestion calibrated to your unconscious preferences. These aren't the by-products of technology—they are the intended output. Microtargeting has moved from marketing novelty to an infrastructural principle of the digital world. What was once a strategy to sell shoes now imperceptibly reshapes identity, ideology, and patterns of belief. *The most powerful interventions in modern life no longer come in the form of persuasion—but prediction.*

Behavioural targeting doesn't shout. It whispers. The digital trails we leave behind—our clicks, pauses, scrolls, purchases, hesitations—are turned into real-time psychological profiles. These profiles are then matched with content, ads, offers, and nudges crafted not for people like us, but *precisely* for us. No longer does a person choose from a shelf of ideas; the shelf rearranges itself based on who it thinks the person is. This shift, subtle in interaction but profound in implication, has transformed the architecture of autonomy.

One of the most illustrative domains for understanding this shift is political advertising. During the 2016 U.S. presidential election, the political consultancy Cambridge Analytica infamously harvested Facebook data from millions of users to microtarget individuals with emotionally resonant political messaging. The targeting wasn't based on party affiliation but psychographic traits—

such as neuroticism or openness—revealed through digital behaviour. The messages were customised to appeal to fears, biases, or values that the user hadn't necessarily expressed aloud. *This wasn't campaigning; it was behaviourally-driven engineering of sentiment at scale.*

In commercial domains, the same methods drive the recommendation engines of Amazon, YouTube, Spotify, and Instagram. What to buy, what to watch, what to listen to—each decision filtered through behavioural predictions. But the impact extends beyond the act of consumption. What's at stake is not just *what* people choose, but *who* they become through the act of repeatedly choosing within algorithmically curated boundaries. *Identity begins to stabilise around the signals you send, rather than the intentions you hold.*

Personalisation, in this context, often masquerades as empowerment. You are given more of what you "like," offered more of what aligns with your inferred desires, and shown what's deemed relevant to you. But relevance is rarely neutral. The very act of determining what is relevant involves assumptions about value, importance, and identity. If a person watches a documentary on climate change, is their interest intellectual, emotional, political? The system doesn't ask—it decides. Future recommendations are shaped not by a person's conscious intentions but by probabilistic interpretations of past behaviour. *The more a system predicts, the more it prescribes.*

There's a creeping circularity here. Targeted systems observe your actions, infer your preferences, then shape future environments to reinforce those preferences. The more one clicks on a certain kind of news story, the more one sees that kind of story, until alternative views are edged out—not through censorship, but *through omission.* A worldview forms not by exploration, but by subtle reinforcement. Over time, belief systems harden—not necessarily because people become more radical, but because the terrain of alternative perspectives becomes algorithmically invisible.

In such systems, the line between feedback and manipulation becomes indistinct. Traditional advertising operated through overt appeal—you knew you were being sold to. But microtargeting operates beneath awareness. A shift in colour, a minor change in font, a nudge in phrasing, a sequence of content—all imperceptible adjustments guided by models that anticipate behaviour. And these systems improve through reinforcement. If you respond positively, the model is validated; if not, it tries again. It doesn't need to understand you. It needs only to *predict* you. And in prediction, it subtly reshapes you.

Platforms often frame this as enhancing user experience. After all, who doesn't want content tailored to their tastes? But the tailoring is not for your benefit alone. Behind every "recommended for you" label lies a network of commercial and ideological interests. What's predicted to work best for you is also what's most profitable for the platform. Aligning user engagement with platform incentives creates a feedback loop in which personalisation serves both as customer service and strategic manipulation. *Convenience becomes a Trojan horse for control.*

There is also a political dimension to this machinery. Microtargeting doesn't just sell things; it sells narratives. When political ads are shown to different users with different messages—based on what each individual is most likely to find persuasive—it fragments the public sphere. Two citizens in the same democracy may receive contradictory accounts of reality, tailored to their biases. Deliberation falters when there is no shared informational ground. *A society nudged in millions of directions cannot easily engage in collective reasoning.*

Yet to critique microtargeting is not to romanticise the past. Mass media, too, shaped beliefs—just more crudely. Newspaper editorial lines, broadcast agendas, and public relations campaigns all exerted their own forms of narrative control. What distinguishes microtargeting is not intent, but precision. *The shift from message to model—from persuasion to prediction—marks a qualitative transformation in how influence operates.*

Resistance, therefore, cannot take the form of disengagement alone. One can log off Facebook or turn off recommendations, but the infrastructure of behavioural targeting permeates countless digital touchpoints: banking apps, news feeds, job platforms, navigation services, even dating profiles. The future of autonomy may depend less on opting out, and more on demanding transparency in *how* preferences are inferred, *why* particular content is shown, and *who* ultimately benefits from those choices.

There are emerging attempts to mitigate these effects. Regulations like the EU's General Data Protection Regulation (GDPR) include provisions for data transparency and algorithmic accountability. Some platforms have introduced controls that let users "tune" their feed. But these solutions often require a level of user attention and digital literacy that is inconsistent at best. Moreover, they tend to treat microtargeting as a privacy issue, rather than a deeper problem of epistemic and ideological autonomy. *What you are shown is inseparable from what you can imagine.*

Ultimately, microtargeting exposes a deeper tension between efficiency and selfhood. Personalisation offers speed, relevance, convenience—but at what cost to serendipity, to exposure, to change? The irony is sharp: by making decisions easier, platforms make them less our own. By reducing friction, they reduce reflection. *The more you are known, the less you are free to become something new.*

To confront the implications of behavioural targeting is not merely to critique a business model—it is to ask what kind of selves we are becoming under its influence. It is to recognise that the architecture of the digital world is not neutral ground, but a terrain sculpted to guide, nudge, and mould. If identity is shaped by what one repeatedly does, and what one does is shaped by what one is repeatedly shown, then the politics of visibility—the hidden logic of who sees what—becomes the politics of personhood itself.

The Illusion of Self-Direction

Freedom, as commonly conceived in liberal democracies, rests on the assumption of choice. We imagine ourselves as self-authored beings—agents who deliberate, decide, and direct the course of our lives. Yet in the personalised digital environments that increasingly shape our actions, this foundational belief is quietly eroded. Personalisation—sold as a tool for empowerment—functions more like a mirror held up to the past. Its logic is not to challenge you, but to confirm you. And in doing so, it subtly closes the door to novelty, growth, and even dissent. *The self that personalisation reflects is not the self you could become, but the one you've already been.*

At the core of this paradox lies a feedback loop disguised as freedom. Recommendation engines, predictive feeds, curated playlists, targeted ads, and custom content—all these mechanisms are designed to align with your preferences. But preferences, in this context, are algorithmically distilled from historical data: what you clicked, watched, paused on, liked, bought, or ignored. The system then offers you more of what it infers you want. This is not an inherently malicious design. On the surface, it optimises convenience, reduces search costs, and caters to relevance. But *relevance,* as defined by algorithms, is often regressive. It assumes that what you did yesterday should shape what you see today.

Netflix might know which documentaries you're statistically likely to finish. Spotify might predict the next song you'll play. TikTok might refine your feed with eerie speed. But what is rarely asked is *why* those patterns are considered normative, or *what alternative experiences* are being screened out. Because every algorithmic decision is a decision not just about what to show—but about what *not* to show. And in the accumulation of these omissions lies a deeper cost: the progressive narrowing of possibility.

This mechanism has been termed "filtering by familiarity," where systems default to offering users the path of least resistance: content that aligns with known tastes, behaviours, or beliefs. This logic is self-reinforcing. If a user shows interest in a particular aesthetic, worldview, or genre, the system serves more of it. But rarely is the boundary pushed. Why offer a jazz listener a Renaissance choral piece? Why introduce a feminist reader to traditionalist critiques? From the perspective of the system, deviation equals risk. *Novelty is algorithmically expensive. Predictability is profitable.*

The result is what we might call *the comfort trap*. Personalisation doesn't coerce—it cocoons. It creates an environment in which users feel more "seen" while actually being less exposed to the unfamiliar. On an individual level, this may seem benign. But scaled across millions of users, it fosters a culture of frictionless self-reinforcement, in which the incentive to explore, rethink, or resist is weakened. You are encouraged not to experiment, but to double down.

This has wide-ranging implications for self-development. Human growth has historically been tethered to disruption: the difficult book, the unexpected conversation, the disorienting encounter with an unfamiliar idea. These are not always pleasant experiences—but they are often transformative. By contrast, personalisation prioritises *pleasantness*. The easiest content, the smoothest UX, the most agreeable ideas—these are pushed forward not because they're best, but because they're least likely to cause dissonance. *Personalisation rewards comfort over confrontation, affirmation over ambiguity.*

And yet, the interface whispers otherwise. It frames its recommendations as empowering: *You may also like…* or *Because you watched…* or *Tailored for you*. The user feels in control, when in fact their choices are pre-structured by a logic that aims not to expand agency, but to extend engagement. The irony is sharp: systems built to serve you increasingly shape you, all while convincing you that you are making the choices.

In behavioural economics, there's a distinction between *System 1* and *System 2* thinking: the former is fast, intuitive, and automatic; the latter is slow, deliberative, and effortful. Personalised environments overwhelmingly cater to System 1. They minimise cognitive strain, shorten decision paths, and capitalise on impulsive behaviours. While this offers speed and satisfaction, it also displaces reflection. You don't pause to question the next video because it auto-plays. You don't explore alternatives because the feed scrolls endlessly. *The environment conditions your behaviour, then calls it preference.*

This conditioning is not confined to entertainment. In domains such as job searching, housing, healthcare, or education, algorithmic personalisation can entrench social inequalities. If past browsing behaviour or demographic profiles lead certain users to be shown fewer high-paying jobs or fewer loan options, then personalisation becomes a tool for social stratification. The illusion of choice masks the reality of exclusion. *What looks like agency from within may be discrimination from above.*

Even when personalisation is less overtly harmful, it can still shape identities in subtle ways. A teenager whose feed reinforces a single political ideology may come to believe that opposition is irrational. A person interested in fitness might slowly adopt hyper-competitive or body-obsessive norms. A new parent could be funnelled into consumption patterns they never actively chose. In each case, the path is not coerced—but it is *scaffolded.* Options appear that confirm the self, rather than challenge it. And over time, *the scaffolding becomes the structure.*

Some technologists argue that personalisation is simply a tool—that its impact depends on how it's used. And in narrow terms, this is true. Not all recommendation systems are equally myopic. Some allow for serendipity. Others intentionally inject variation. But the dominant commercial logic remains aligned with retention, not revelation. Algorithms are tuned to keep users engaged, not enlightened. And engagement thrives on predictability, not surprise.

There is, of course, no returning to a pre-personalised digital world. Nor should there be. Personalisation can offer real benefits: accessibility, efficiency, reduced overload. But *the terms of engagement must be reimagined.* Transparency must increase—users should know not just what is shown, but why. Systems must allow for friction—space for disagreement, error, or curiosity. And users must be invited into practices of self-awareness: not just *what do I want?* but *why do I want it?* and *who shaped that wanting?*

The deeper task is cultural as much as technical. We need to reclaim discomfort as a site of growth. We need to value cognitive diversity, not just ideological echo. We need to resist the seductions of smoothness that reduce identity to a series of behavioural breadcrumbs. *True agency requires not just options, but awareness of how those options came to be.*

To believe we are self-directed in a world designed to guide us invisibly is not just naïve—it is dangerous. It undermines the conditions for meaningful autonomy, for collective deliberation, for genuine change. The illusion of self-direction, if left unchallenged, becomes a reality of quiet compliance. And the cost is not merely personal. It is political, epistemic, and existential. A society of users comforted into complacency is one that gradually forgets how to question, how to imagine, how to choose.

The Cost of Frictionlessness

Efficiency has long been equated with progress. The drive to eliminate barriers, shorten decision paths, and streamline user experience has become the organising principle of the digital economy. From one-click ordering to auto-filled logins, from predictive search to biometric paywalls, our interactions with technology are being continuously refined for speed. The term 'frictionless'—once a metaphor borrowed from physics—is now a design imperative. But beneath its polished appeal lies a deeper, less examined cost: *what is removed when effort disappears?* When systems pre-empt our intention, when choices are made easier by making them less conscious, what happens to reflection, agency, or the space for moral or social deliberation?

In psychological terms, friction is not merely a nuisance. It can be a signal. It slows us down, invites us to reconsider, to weigh alternatives, to connect action with consequence. Yet many digital platforms treat friction as an enemy of engagement. Amazon's "Buy Now" button bypasses the shopping cart entirely. Instagram enables story sharing with a single swipe. TikTok loads the next video without asking if the viewer wants it. These are not marginal improvements; they are *strategic reductions in deliberation.* And they work precisely because they anticipate—and override—hesitation.

Consider how checkout processes have evolved. A decade ago, buying something online required at least a few steps: product selection, cart review, address confirmation, payment entry. Each was a potential moment for reconsideration. Now, with saved payment credentials and frictionless pathways, purchases are often complete within seconds. What was once a decision is now a gesture. This shift may feel benign, even convenient, but the psychology is revealing. *Removing effort also removes the cues that trigger reflection.* Users are less likely to ask: "Do I really need this?" because there is no longer a natural pause in which that question might arise.

The consequences of this aren't limited to commerce. They extend into politics, relationships, attention, and belief. Frictionless retweets enable outrage to spread faster than the truth can catch up. Quick likes become social currency in shallow economies of affirmation. Default autoplay features ensure that viewers keep watching, often without intending to. The user's will is not actively suppressed—it is simply circumvented. *Agency becomes passive. Consent becomes ambient.*

One of the most overlooked effects of frictionless design is how it reshapes the architecture of decision-making. Classical models of rational choice assume that people weigh costs and benefits. But such models depend on *time*—and friction is what buys that time. In the absence of friction, decisions are offloaded to impulse. This has ethical implications. A user swiping through personalised dating profiles is less likely to treat others as subjects and more as consumable content. A reader scrolling headlines might react to provocations without context. A viewer binge-watching content at 2 a.m. may override sleep, not out of preference, but out of momentum. *Frictionlessness fosters a kind of learned autopilot.*

Some may argue that removing effort enhances inclusion. After all, not everyone has the same bandwidth, cognitive resources, or digital fluency. In domains such as accessibility, reduced friction can be empowering. Voice-to-text tools, predictive typing, and simplified interfaces do make certain tasks more navigable. But there is a key difference between *designing for accessibility* and *designing for addiction*. The former is a form of justice. The latter is a form of subtle coercion. *When design decisions are optimised for engagement above all else, convenience becomes a cover for control.*

An instructive case lies in the rise of default settings. Behavioural economists have long documented the power of defaults. In countries where citizens are automatically enrolled in organ donor programmes (with the option to opt out), participation rates are significantly higher than in opt-in systems. The lesson is not that people are more altruistic in one country than another—but that default paths shape behaviour, often invisibly. In the digital sphere, frictionless defaults are everywhere. Autoplay is on. Notifications are enabled. Location tracking is active. Opting out requires effort—adding friction. Opting in requires nothing at all. The result is that *what happens by default is often mistaken for what users truly want.*

This has led to a conceptual confusion between preference and path dependence. Just because a user clicks on a link, watches a video, or accepts a recommendation does not mean that was their original intent. It may simply have been the smoothest path. But when systems are built to interpret interaction as endorsement, they become increasingly skilled at reinforcing the same paths. Over time, this doesn't just influence *what* users choose. It influences *how* they think. *Frictionless design is not just about interface; it is about ideology. It privileges immediate satisfaction over considered judgment.*

There is an economic rationale for this. Platforms are in the business of time capture. The more time users spend on a site, the more data is collected, the more ads are served, the more money is made. Friction is the enemy of that model. A button that requires confirmation, a step that requires a pause, a prompt that demands thought—all of these slow down the cycle. So platforms have engineered them away. But in doing so, they have eroded what makes decisions *meaningful*: the struggle, however minor, to *choose deliberately*.

The irony is that frictionless systems often feel more empowering. They present themselves as liberators from complexity. But the power they offer is superficial. Real power lies in understanding the context of one's choices, in being able to reflect, resist, or revise. A system that anticipates your needs and acts on your behalf without asking doesn't empower you—it infantilises you. *It replaces sovereignty with surrender, awareness with automation.*

To be clear, not all friction is good. Bureaucratic delays, clunky interfaces, and poorly designed tools waste time and create barriers. But there is a profound difference between *unnecessary effort* and *necessary pause*. The former is an obstacle. The latter is a feature. *Deliberation is not inefficiency. It is a cornerstone of autonomy.*

The challenge, then, is not to eliminate friction but to *design it intentionally*. Ethical design must reintroduce slowness in places where speed obscures consequence. It must build prompts for reflection into systems that otherwise invite reflex. It must make visible the hidden levers of influence and offer users genuine agency—not just over what they choose, but over how those choices are presented.

This may mean adding confirmation steps before irreversible actions. It may mean pausing autoplay after a set number of episodes. It may mean designing algorithms that prioritise diversity over familiarity, ambiguity over certainty. It may even mean acknowledging that some of the best decisions are the ones that *take time. Friction is not the enemy of the user. It is the ally of the human.*

Design is never neutral. The structure of choice influences the shape of thought. And thought, in turn, shapes society. A culture built on frictionless interaction may move faster—but it does not necessarily move better. It risks becoming a culture of immediacy without memory, of convenience without conscience. And in such a culture, the very capacity to pause, to reconsider, to say no—to *choose differently*—begins to wither.

We must ask, then, not just what our technologies allow us to do, but what they encourage us to *become*. If we are constantly nudged into now—into the next click, the next video, the next task—when do we get to stop and ask whether the direction is right? Friction is how we regain that moment. It is how we insert ourselves back into the loop. And it is, perhaps, the last defence against a future where every action is automatic, and every decision is already made.

From Influence to Infrastructure

Most nudges are invisible. That is their design. Whether it's the placement of a default toggle, the suggestion of "people you may know," or the auto-selection of the shortest route home, subtle cues embedded into digital systems now direct billions of decisions per day. These micro-interventions were once conceptualised as benevolent behavioural nudges—light touches on the cognitive tiller that help people make better choices, or at least choices aligned with their stated goals. But today's nudging isn't just an act of design; it's a condition of the environment. *What began as influence has ossified into infrastructure.*

The concept of nudging entered popular discourse through behavioural economics, most notably the work of Richard Thaler and Cass Sunstein, who advocated for "choice architecture" that could gently steer decisions without eliminating freedom. The classic example: rearranging a cafeteria so that healthier foods appear first. It's still possible to choose the cookie—but the salad is made more accessible. Transposed into the digital realm, however, the scale and persistence of nudging mechanisms change the equation. They don't merely present a better option. They *repeatedly pre-condition choice environments* in ways that shape perception, preference, and even identity over time.

To understand the gravity of this shift, one must stop viewing nudging as a single point of influence and start seeing it as a distributed system of conditioning. Platforms like Facebook, YouTube, and TikTok do not just nudge users into selecting particular content—they embed those nudges into the very mechanisms through which content is discovered, interpreted, and reinforced. If the cafeteria layout is reconfigured several times a day based on what the eater previously consumed—if the signage, lighting, and pathways all subtly adjust to maximise calorie intake—then at some point, the eater is not choosing within an environment. They are *being shaped by it.*

This is what makes digital nudging structurally distinct from its analog predecessors. It is *not episodic but continuous.* It is not designed once and left in place, but perpetually recalibrated based on telemetry, attention, and past interaction. The system doesn't simply show the salad first—it begins to define what counts as a salad, what is visible, what is normal, and what is desirable. *Personalisation becomes predestination.* The architecture of choice becomes a closed loop.

Consider the case of Netflix. When users open the app, they are met with a preview that auto-plays before they have made any selections. Thumbnails are algorithmically chosen based on what the user has previously watched—not just genre or actors, but emotional tone and visual framing. Over time, the interface itself adapts to the user's inferred desires. This isn't coercion in the traditional sense. Users can still search manually. But most don't. *The majority of views come from surface-level suggestions.* The system has learned how to get ahead of intention. The user feels autonomous because they clicked play. But the environment did most of the deciding.

What's more, this environment is not passive. It is responsive, self-updating, and commercially motivated. Nudging has become a revenue model. Platforms optimise for engagement, not wellbeing. They know which thumbnails convert, which headlines provoke outrage, which products benefit from impulse clicks. Over time, these nudges aren't just pushing users toward specific outcomes—they are *training users to become the kinds of people who consistently produce those outcomes.* A user who repeatedly responds to political fearbait is nudged toward more of it, and gradually begins to think in its terms. *Nudging becomes norming.*

This feedback loop is what elevates nudging to the level of infrastructure. Infrastructure does not ask for attention. It organises it. Infrastructure does not need to argue for itself. It frames the conversation. Sidewalks shape foot traffic. Road widths influence speed. Electrical grids determine which homes receive power first after a storm. Digital nudging is no different—it's just less visible. The default notification settings on smartphones determine which messages are seen instantly and which are missed for hours. The suggested replies in Gmail influence tone and brevity. Autocomplete finishes our sentences. *And every subtle assist accumulates into a worldview: fast, curated, affirming, and frictionless.*

This infrastructural turn matters because it changes how we think about responsibility. If influence is a tactic, then designers and engineers are merely crafting better tools. If nudging is infrastructure, then they are *governing environments.* The ethics are no longer about single interactions but systemic outcomes. Is it ethical for a music streaming service to push artists it has a financial stake in, using opaque algorithms that suppress others? Is it ethical for a navigation app to route drivers through residential streets without residents' consent, purely for efficiency? These are not interface questions. They are questions about governance, legitimacy, and democratic oversight.

One of the most instructive developments in this space is the rise of "dark patterns"—interface designs that manipulate users into decisions they might not otherwise make. These include hidden opt-outs, pre-checked boxes, misleading button labelling, and more. Regulatory bodies are beginning to push back. The UK's Information Commissioner's Office has issued guidance on age-appropriate design. The EU's Digital Services Act is targeting algorithmic transparency. But these measures address the most egregious cases. *They don't yet touch the deeper truth: that the entire digital ecosystem is built on structural nudging.*

It's important not to reduce this critique to dystopian alarmism. Nudging as infrastructure is not inherently bad. It can be used to support attention, promote healthier behaviours, or elevate underrepresented voices. A news aggregator that intentionally diversifies sources is still nudging, but toward epistemic richness. A productivity app that delays notifications until a task is complete is nudging for focus. The problem is not nudging per se. *The problem is that users are largely unaware of its presence, its logic, or its direction.*

Agency requires not just freedom of choice but *awareness of the conditions under which choices are made.* The most concerning aspect of infrastructure-level nudging is that it hides its own architecture. Users are rarely informed why a particular ad was served, why a post was prioritised, or why a prompt appeared at a given moment. Without that context, users cannot interrogate or resist the nudge. They are navigating blind. And in a world where most behaviour is digitally mediated, *being blind to the environment is being governed by it.*

One response to this dilemma is the call for algorithmic transparency. But transparency alone is insufficient. Most users won't read disclosure statements or decode neural network logic. What's needed is *interpretability*—designs that help users understand the system's intentions, incentives, and likely trajectories. Think of it as civic literacy for the digital age. Just as citizens must understand laws to participate meaningfully in a democracy, users must understand systems to exercise genuine agency online.

The reframing of nudging as infrastructure invites a more serious reckoning with digital power. It challenges the narrative that users are simply choosing poorly, that better behaviour is a matter of willpower. It suggests instead that *behaviour is downstream of design.* And when design operates at infrastructural scale—pervasive, persistent, and programmable—then choice itself becomes a managed commodity.

In that light, the most urgent questions are not about what we click, but about *who builds the walls around what we can click.* Whose values shape the defaults? Whose interests are served by "recommended for you"? How can users reclaim intentionality in systems designed to anticipate and automate their every move?

Nudging, at this scale, is not a feature. It is a form of governance. And governance demands scrutiny, debate, and accountability. If we fail to see that, we risk mistaking convenience for consent—and design for destiny. Nudging becomes infrastructure the moment it no longer asks for permission, because it no longer needs to. That is the moment we must begin to ask harder questions—not about *whether* we are being influenced, but *how deeply we are already shaped.*

Chapter 5
Automation Anxiety

To hand a task over to automation is to subtly transform its value, shift responsibility, and redefine what it means to be human in relation to it. There is no neutral handover. Whether it is a car switching to self-drive, a calendar proposing your week's schedule, or a chatbot triaging a medical concern, each automated function carries an implicit promise: you no longer need to think about this. Yet the unspoken consequence is that, over time, you may also forget how. As systems increasingly handle complex operations with minimal input, the anxiety is less about whether machines can perform and more about what their performance costs us.

Automation anxiety is not technophobia. It is not a fear that machines will replace humans, but a reckoning with what humans become in the process. The change is philosophical as well as functional. To relinquish control—whether over small decisions or significant ones—is also to relocate agency. Questions arise about cognition, ethics, and identity: when does convenience slip into dependence? When does delegation border on abdication?

Consider the unassuming predictive keyboard. Not long ago, typing on a mobile device demanded deliberate composition. Now, autocomplete anticipates your next word, your sentence, even your tone. The interaction feels seamless, almost invisible. But gradually, reliance on these predictive patterns subtly alters expression. Communication becomes faster, but not necessarily more thoughtful; efficiency begins to outweigh deliberation. The machine does not merely aid communication—it shapes it.

Extend this across the infrastructure of daily life, and the implications become clearer. Self-driving cars minimise human error yet erode spatial awareness and attention. Smart thermostats optimise comfort while abstracting energy literacy. Email filters shield against overload but obscure selection logic. Recommendation engines present the "next best" option, quietly smoothing over the criteria that define "best." Each layer of automation removes friction—and familiarity with the task it performs. To let go of the wheel is to trust a system to navigate in your stead, to unlearn the feel of the road.

Time-saving convenience becomes epistemic displacement. Automation does not simply replace labour; it supplants judgment. As systems improve, dependence grows. And with dependence comes vulnerability: who bears responsibility when a system fails? A self-driving car causes a fatality—manufacturer, coder, passenger? A clinical decision system misclassifies a tumour—can a physician override a confident probability matrix?

These questions are not theoretical. In 2018, a pedestrian was killed by an autonomous Uber in Arizona, despite a safety driver onboard. The system had classified the pedestrian as "other," failing to trigger emergency braking. Responsibility ricocheted between human monitors, engineering limitations, and corporate protocol. The lesson was stark: as decision-making is distributed, ethical frameworks lag. Locating culpability grows ever more complex.

High-stakes environments illustrate this tension sharply. In aviation, pilots supervise systems rather than navigate directly. When these systems fail, human re-entry is often too late or disoriented—the 2009 Air France Flight 447 disaster remains a chilling reminder. In medicine, algorithms assist in triage, imaging, and treatment suggestions. Performance may exceed human capacity in specific tasks, yet the locus of trust shifts. Physicians must discern when to defer and when to intervene, a skill demanding epistemic humility and systems literacy.

Yet the greatest effect of automation is not catastrophic failure but subtle erosion. Intellectual atrophy creeps in as engagement with routine decisions wanes. Behavioural studies show reliance on assistive technologies diminishes confidence and competence. GPS has dulled wayfinding skills; calculators have weakened mental arithmetic. Not inherently damaging, these trends illustrate how delegation often dilutes human capacity.

The promise of automation as liberation—freedom from drudgery and overload—requires nuance. What is forfeited when we no longer engage? Which qualities erode when effort is removed? Friction is where learning occurs, discernment is tested, and character is shaped. Automating judgment reshapes not only what we do but our sense of competence, awareness, and responsibility.

Not all automation is. problematic. Systems managing dangerous or redundant tasks—industrial robots, fire suppression, climate control—enhance safety and productivity. But when automation encroaches on personal agency or moral discretion, stakes rise. A calendar suggesting a break is convenient; a decision engine advising whom to date or which job to apply for crosses into terrain where preferences, values, and aspirations reside. The risk lies not only in poor outcomes but in diminished ownership of life's direction.

Automation rarely declares its scope. It is ambient, embedded, always on. You may not perceive nudging, assistance, or override. Trade-offs, optimisations, and exclusions remain opaque. Choice becomes constrained by invisible architectures shaped by others' priorities. Apparent freedom of choice is compromised when the set of options is preordained.

Navigating this terrain demands discerning delegation from abdication. Delegation is conscious, strategic, transferring tasks to tools to advance goals. Abdication is passive, surrendering agency in exchange for convenience. The line is subtle but consequential, hinging on understanding, consent, and accountability.

This chapter interrogates that boundary, exploring how humans relate to automated systems—not merely in utility but in cognition, ethics, and identity. It asks what is gained and lost when systems decide for us. Can confidence in judgment coexist with technological dependence? What are the philosophical implications of frictionless decision-making in a world where responsibility is diffuse?

Automation anxiety is not a rejection of progress; it signals that something deeper is at stake: our sense of competence, accountability, and discernment. Recognising the hidden trade-offs in a world where letting go of the wheel seems inevitable is not optional—it is essential.

Letting Go of the Wheel

A glance at a Tesla gliding down a motorway without a driver's hands on the wheel might once have symbolised innovation, even liberation. But what precisely is being liberated—and what is being surrendered in its place? As automation weaves itself into the fabric of daily life—from the cars we ride to the emails we answer, from reminders we didn't set to meetings we didn't remember planning—it becomes less a marvel and more a mirror. A mirror that reflects our willingness to relinquish control in exchange for ease, and the slow erosion of decision-making as a lived, felt human experience.

The appeal of automation is rarely debated in terms of philosophy—it's a design feature, not an ethical dilemma. Yet beneath every swipe that sorts our photos, every AI-crafted to-do list, and every auto-suggested navigation route, there lies a silent contract: *we accept cognitive outsourcing as the price of convenience.* The trade-off sounds reasonable in a busy world. Why not delegate the mundane to machines? But the subtlety of what we lose—our awareness, our deliberation, even our sense of authorship over our lives—is not always noticed until it's already gone.

The automobile offers a vivid case study. A driver who once memorised maps and calculated alternate routes now watches passively as an app dictates turns and avoids traffic. When autonomous features like adaptive cruise control or lane keeping take over, reaction times lengthen. Studies from the Insurance Institute for Highway Safety show that drivers of vehicles with partial automation are more likely to disengage—mentally, if not physically—from the task of driving. They check their phones more often. They miss auditory warnings. In short, the human factor begins to blur, yet accountability remains squarely human when errors occur. The machine may steer, but the human is still expected to take the fall.

The psychological impact runs deeper than a diminished reaction time. It touches the core of how people experience agency. Tasks that once demanded focus and attention—navigating traffic, composing emails, choosing routes—now happen invisibly, with the machine offering "smart" defaults that discourage reconsideration. As decisions are made for us, even minor ones, the practice of decision-making atrophies. A daily calendar that pre-emptively prioritises meetings, a music app that queues your "favourites" without asking, a fridge that reorders groceries—all promise optimisation. But optimised for what? Rarely are users prompted to reflect on whether what's easiest is also what's best. *The friction we remove is often the very thing that gives choices their depth and weight.*

Automation often blurs the line between delegation and abdication. Delegation is a choice; it implies oversight and retrieval. Abdication is the opposite: it quietly allows responsibility to drift into the background, unrecalled and unchallenged. Consider the proliferation of smart assistants. They schedule meetings, rebook flights, adjust thermostats. Users interact via voice, issuing commands without thought to the broader architecture driving those commands. There is no neutral technology here. Each suggestion, default, and automation path is shaped by institutional priorities—be they those of a tech firm, advertiser, or productivity platform. This means that "letting go of the wheel" rarely means letting go into a void. It's a handoff, often to systems shaped by opaque objectives.

In healthcare, the implications are more profound. Diagnostic algorithms increasingly assist doctors by highlighting likely conditions or recommending treatment pathways based on pattern recognition across large datasets. These tools save time and reduce oversight. But they also risk deskilling practitioners over time, encouraging deference to the machine rather than patient nuance. When a physician trusts a predictive model without questioning its assumptions, does she still practise medicine—or merely facilitate protocol?

Or consider the growing use of predictive policing software, which identifies "high-risk" zones or individuals based on past data. The system may claim impartiality, but its logic perpetuates historic biases baked into the data. Officers following these nudges may believe they are simply responding to intelligence. In truth, they are reinforcing the past while believing they are acting in the present.

Even the seemingly benign realm of personal scheduling reveals troubling shifts. Digital calendars that suggest meeting times, auto-fill availability, and sync seamlessly with others reduce the friction of coordination—but also erode spontaneous interactions, unstructured time, and the minor but meaningful negotiations that make scheduling a shared activity. This isn't merely about efficiency. It's about the quiet disappearance of relational texture in favour of logistical symmetry. When every gap in time becomes a target for insertion, life becomes a calendar to be managed, not a rhythm to be lived.

What automation quietly edits out is not just effort, but reflection. The pause before a decision. The second thought. The alternate path. Automation makes sense when it removes burden; it becomes problematic when it removes deliberation. This shift from conscious choice to guided completion may not feel dramatic. In fact, it rarely does. But this subtlety is its strength—and our vulnerability.

The irony is that while automation often markets itself as empowering the individual, it does so by replacing that individual's judgment with pre-solved pathways. This contradiction is not a flaw of design—it's its central feature. It allows people to feel more efficient, more responsive, even more independent, while relying increasingly on systems they neither control nor fully understand.

The net result is a society that feels more capable and less competent. Decisions happen faster, but understanding dwindles. The ability to intervene, to override, to deviate from the default—all critical facets of autonomy—are less practised, and therefore less available. And when automation fails, as it inevitably does, the resulting disorientation is not just technical—it is existential. *What do you do when you've forgotten how to choose for yourself?*

The future promises more of this. Autonomous vehicles, smart cities, predictive hiring algorithms, adaptive education platforms—all offer efficiencies. But as humans recede from the loop, a fundamental question emerges: *What kind of person do we become when we no longer need to navigate complexity, weigh options, or tolerate ambiguity?*

To be clear, this is not a call for technophobia or regression. It is a call for conscious engagement. Automation can be profoundly useful. But it should be visible, interruptible, and accountable. The systems that drive our lives should not be allowed to drift from tools to terrains—unchosen, unexamined, and unresisted. *Letting go of the wheel may feel like progress, but only if we remember where we're going—and how to take back the wheel when we must.*

Delegation vs. Abdication

On the surface, automation promises liberation: less effort, fewer decisions, more time. But not all delegation is created equal. What begins as convenience can evolve—often imperceptibly—into abdication, where human judgement is not merely assisted but displaced. This distinction is not philosophical hair-splitting; in high-stakes environments, the difference can be decisive. When a clinician follows a diagnostic algorithm without second-guessing it, or when a pilot relies entirely on autopilot without monitoring its outputs, the shift from delegation to abdication is no longer abstract—it becomes operational, and potentially catastrophic. *Frictionless convenience can quietly corrode our vigilance.*

Consider aviation, a domain long used as a model for human-machine coordination. After the 2009 crash of Air France Flight 447, investigators highlighted a concerning trend: over-reliance on autopilot systems had led to the atrophy of manual flying skills among pilots. The crew, faced with a sudden disengagement of automation in turbulent conditions, responded with confusion and conflicting inputs. The pilots, trained professionals, were not incompetent—they were simply out of practice, cognitively distant from a skill now mostly outsourced. The system, intended to reduce workload, had instead eroded essential competencies. *Delegation had become abdication, and the cost was irreversible.*

This erosion of skill is neither limited to rarefied domains like aviation nor marked by dramatic failures. It plays out quietly in the everyday tools of modern professionals. Consider financial advisors using robo-advisors or algorithmic forecasting tools. Initially meant to enhance decision-making by crunching numbers and identifying trends, these platforms can begin to supplant judgement if the professional ceases to challenge their assumptions. When the model suggests reallocating a client's assets based on risk scores, does the advisor still scrutinise the logic behind it? Or does the glossy dashboard and consistent performance metrics create a false sense of infallibility?

The psychological seduction is subtle but strong. Delegation requires oversight—an active relationship between human and tool. Abdication, by contrast, is passive. It transfers responsibility to the system. This shift is reinforced by *design choices that promote trust without transparency*: interfaces that highlight simplicity over explainability, alerts that assume binary decisions, recommendations that suppress alternative paths. In these environments, asking too many questions can feel inefficient, even deviant. Efficiency becomes not just a goal but a discipline, punishing dissent.

This is not an argument against automation. Rather, it's a call to reinstate human agency within the automated loop. The crucial task is not to resist automation but to *redefine the boundaries of meaningful delegation*. In healthcare, clinical decision support systems are often framed as second opinions. But research has shown that when systems output a clear directive—"Treat with X"—practitioners are less likely to consider nuanced factors like comorbidities, lifestyle, or patient preference. The machine is not wrong; it is merely incomplete. Delegation, in this case, requires that the clinician retain the role of integrator, not merely executor.

A similar dynamic emerges in law enforcement. Predictive policing algorithms purport to identify high-risk individuals or neighbourhoods. Officers, understandably stretched thin, might treat these predictions as mandates. Over time, discretionary judgement—the core of ethical policing—can be replaced by data-driven directives. The system does not simply inform strategy; it begins to dictate it. The risk is twofold: not only might the data reflect existing biases, but the officers themselves may lose the reflex to question it. *Delegation becomes dependence. Dependence becomes doctrine.*

What makes this shift particularly insidious is that it rarely feels like surrender. Unlike a top-down directive or a coerced order, abdication via automation often feels like a favour—like being helped. The system takes over scheduling meetings, suggesting replies, prompting decisions. And in so doing, it shapes the rhythm and structure of thought itself. Research in cognitive psychology has demonstrated that *humans are natural satisficers*—we tend to settle for "good enough" answers, especially under time pressure. Automated tools amplify this tendency by surfacing pre-selected, optimised choices that feel authoritative. When Google auto-completes a search query or when Netflix recommends your next show, the ease is gratifying. The alternatives you might have chosen remain invisible. Over time, the boundary between help and hegemony blurs.

Crucially, the distinction between delegation and abdication lies not in the system's sophistication, but in *the user's stance toward it.* Delegation implies retaining ownership over the outcome. It is a mode of partnership, one that allows for override, doubt, and discretion. Abdication is characterised by surrender—not of labour, but of responsibility. It is what happens when we not only accept help but cease to imagine alternatives to it.

High-stakes environments magnify the risks of this shift, but they do not create them. Even in mundane digital spaces—calendars, recommendation engines, workflow automation—abdication can shape behaviour in profound ways. Take the case of email scheduling tools. Initially meant to reduce back-and-forth, they now nudge users toward specific time slots or standardised meeting durations. What looks like convenience can, over time, regiment interpersonal dynamics, subtly privileging speed over deliberation, standardisation over nuance. The cost is not simply cognitive; it is cultural.

Part of the solution lies in *designing for deliberation*. Rather than systems that streamline away uncertainty, we need systems that make room for it—interfaces that expose model logic, dashboards that show uncertainty ranges, defaults that encourage rather than replace decision-making. In critical applications like AI-assisted legal sentencing or automated medical triage, this principle is not optional; it is foundational. Transparency must not be treated as a compliance checkbox, but as a cognitive affordance—something that supports, rather than supplants, human agency.

Education, too, plays a role. Training users—whether pilots, doctors, or everyday professionals—to think with machines, rather than through them, is essential. This means cultivating habits of second-guessing, sense-checking, and contextual awareness. Delegation should be taught as a skill, not assumed as an inevitability. The goal is not resistance to automation but fluency with it—a mode of literacy that recognises both its benefits and its boundaries.

Perhaps the most powerful corrective, however, is cultural. We need a shift in how we valorise decision-making. In many professional contexts, speed and consistency are lionised. But true judgement is often slow, hesitant, and iterative. *Delegation that preserves the space for such judgement is healthy. Abdication that forecloses it is not.* The more we romanticise seamlessness, the more we risk losing the very friction that makes decisions ours.

To reclaim that friction is not to regress but to advance—to insist that the future of human-machine collaboration is not just about what machines can do, but about what we refuse to relinquish. This is the crux of the modern digital compact: to delegate wisely, not blindly; to automate with awareness, not abdication. The tools are evolving. The question is whether our judgment is keeping up.

The Quiet Drift Toward Dependence

The most transformative technologies do not arrive with alarms and flashing lights. They are not declared revolutions; they are woven quietly into the routines of everyday life. This is precisely the case with automation. From smart thermostats to autocomplete functions, from tailored playlists to calendar nudges, automated systems increasingly relieve us of small decisions. They promise ease, speed, and precision. But beneath this layer of convenience lies a less examined trade-off: the gradual erosion of confidence in our own judgment. Over time, *what we outsource becomes what we forget how to do*—and what we stop trusting ourselves to decide.

The human brain evolved to be a predictive machine. It constantly assesses, weighs, and adjusts in response to uncertain environments. It thrives on feedback loops, learns from error, and improves through iteration. But automated systems intervene in that loop. They filter complexity, present optimised paths, and remove the friction of uncertainty. While this feels efficient—and often is—it subtly changes the cognitive terrain. Decision-making becomes something we no longer inhabit, but passively receive. The competence we gain through trial and discernment begins to dull, like a muscle left unused.

This drift is not the result of a single device or app, but the cumulative effect of design choices that treat autonomy as expendable. Consider the proliferation of recommendation engines. Whether selecting a film on Netflix or a restaurant via Google Maps, we are gently nudged toward options "for you." These nudges are rarely questioned because they seem helpful. Yet with each instance, the range of conscious deliberation narrows. The act of choosing becomes one of accepting the suggestion, not evaluating it. Over time, we internalise that guidance as superior to our own exploratory impulses.

The loss here is not merely practical—it is epistemic. To know is not only to store information, but to arrive at conclusions through a process of weighing, comparing, and revising. Automation truncates this process. What begins as cognitive delegation morphs into dependence when we no longer feel confident navigating the domain unaided. In domains such as driving, we can see this shift most clearly. Drivers accustomed to GPS guidance often find themselves lost without it, even in familiar places. This is not just about forgetting routes—it reflects a larger disuse of spatial memory, orientation skills, and navigational reasoning.

A similar pattern unfolds in scheduling. Digital calendars that auto-suggest meeting times or propose "focus hours" are doing more than assisting—they're beginning to *shape the rhythm of the day*. When routines become pre-filled and reminders become mandates, our sense of agency over time management changes. We feel efficient, but subtly disoriented when asked to plan without the tool. The psychological phenomenon at play here resembles learned helplessness, except not born of failure—but of passive habituation to optimisation.

There is also an affective consequence. Confidence is not built by always being correct; it is built through the process of working things out. The discomfort of uncertainty, the cognitive load of decision-making, and even the missteps along the way are foundational to resilient reasoning. Automated systems, in relieving us of this burden, interrupt the very process by which individuals mature as thinkers.

When the algorithm gets it wrong—a misfired calendar suggestion, an irrelevant product ad—we're not frustrated merely by inefficiency. We're caught off guard by the sudden requirement to decide unaided. It feels, oddly, like a burden, when it should feel like a baseline.

The commercial incentives behind this drift are powerful. Frictionless interaction means more engagement, quicker conversions, and lower drop-off rates. But what is efficient for platforms may be enfeebling for users. When friction is engineered out of systems, reflection is often engineered out as well. The user is carried along a pre-optimised path, shielded from pauses that might prompt reconsideration. *Deliberation is treated as delay.* In this environment, dependence is not forced—it's designed.

One must distinguish here between productive delegation and passive abdication. Delegation is an act of choice; it involves discernment about which tasks are appropriate to outsource and under what conditions. Abdication, by contrast, is a retreat from responsibility—often masked as convenience. For example, using a grammar tool to catch typos is delegation; letting it choose your phrasing entirely, without review, is abdication. The line between the two is thin, but the psychological outcomes differ dramatically. Delegation empowers by creating bandwidth; abdication erodes confidence by diminishing skill.

Nowhere is this drift more consequential than in high-stakes or knowledge-intensive contexts. In healthcare, clinicians increasingly rely on algorithmic decision support tools. While these systems can flag errors and optimise diagnoses, they can also lead to automation bias—where users over-trust the system even in the face of contradictory evidence. Studies in aviation show similar patterns. Pilots accustomed to autopilot functions demonstrate slower reaction times and weaker situational awareness when manual control is suddenly required. In both cases, automation becomes a cognitive crutch—reliable until it isn't, and paralysing when it fails.

The quietest cost of this dependence may be motivational. When decisions are continuously pre-structured, individuals stop cultivating the internal frameworks needed to make choices confidently. The drive to improve, explore, or even question defaults diminishes. Without awareness, we become flatter versions of ourselves—efficient, perhaps, but hollowed out in the faculties that distinguish reflective humans from obedient users. And this, ultimately, is the paradox of automation: *the very systems that promise to free us from decision fatigue may be making us less capable of making decisions at all.*

Recovering that capability does not require rejecting technology, but rethinking its role. Tools should serve to extend human judgment, not replace it. They should scaffold learning, not displace it. This means designing interfaces that reintroduce moments of pause, that make the path visible rather than invisible, and that invite interaction rather than automate away intention. It also means educating users to recognise when they are choosing—and when they are being carried.

Dependence rarely announces itself. It accrues through thousands of tiny interactions, each one too trivial to notice, until the aggregate reshapes perception, confidence, and ultimately identity. A calendar that thinks for you, a feed that fills itself, a route that chooses you back—all offer ease. But ease without engagement invites erosion. It is not the automation of tasks that should concern us, but the automation of thought. *The more we are guided, the less we remember how to guide ourselves.* And unless that drift is named, it cannot be resisted.

Who's Accountable When No One's Driving?

In March 2018, a self-driving Uber vehicle struck and killed a pedestrian in Tempe, Arizona—the first recorded death of a human being by an autonomous car. The backup driver was distracted. The car's software detected the pedestrian but failed to classify her as a hazard in time. Uber's system had disengaged its emergency braking feature. The tragedy raised a question that is still unsettled today: *Who is at fault when a machine is making the decisions?* The answer isn't merely legal—it's ethical, institutional, and philosophical. As intelligent systems increasingly operate independently in high-stakes environments, we're forced to reckon with a basic problem: when no one is holding the wheel, accountability doesn't disappear. It disperses, evades, and refracts into silence.

The rise of autonomous systems—cars that steer themselves, medical software that diagnoses disease, algorithms that screen job candidates or determine loan eligibility—has not eliminated human influence. It has *diffused* it. Responsibility no longer falls cleanly on the individual developer, operator, or user. Instead, we confront a blurry network of partial control, indirect oversight, and systemic delegation. The traditional legal model of accountability, which requires identifying a liable party, struggles to cope with this ambient decision-making environment. In this new landscape, *automation doesn't absolve responsibility; it complicates its distribution.*

This isn't a speculative concern. Consider the use of algorithmic triage systems in healthcare. In 2020, a major hospital network in the United States deployed an AI tool to help prioritise patients for COVID-19 treatment. The model, trained on historical data, inadvertently underprioritised Black patients due to systemic biases embedded in the data it learned from. No individual set out to engineer this disparity. Yet the outcome was real, measurable, and ethically significant. When the harm emerges from an automated process, who do we hold accountable—the developers, the data scientists, the clinicians who relied on the tool, or the institution that deployed it?

Legal scholars have attempted to keep pace. Some have proposed that AI systems be granted limited forms of "electronic personhood," allowing them to bear legal liability. Others argue for expanding corporate responsibility structures, holding companies strictly liable for damages caused by their autonomous systems regardless of fault. Yet neither approach satisfies the deeper moral unease: *Responsibility is more than blame—it is the duty to be responsive to the impact of one's actions.* And in systems governed by code rather than conscience, responsiveness is neither guaranteed nor demanded.

Part of the difficulty lies in the human tendency to defer to technology. Studies on "automation bias" show that people are prone to over-trust algorithmic outputs, even when they contradict better judgement. In aviation, this has led to fatal consequences: both the 2009 Air France Flight 447 crash and the 2013 Asiana Airlines crash in San Francisco were partially attributed to pilot overreliance on automated flight systems, followed by delayed or confused human intervention. As the cockpit fills with software, the pilot's role becomes more ambiguous—not eliminated, but increasingly latent until crisis demands rapid action. The same dynamic is now playing out across industries.

Crucially, *the issue is not the absence of human input, but the restructuring of human roles*. Rather than removing people from decision-making, automation often relocates them into oversight or exception management roles. But these roles require different skills—ones that are often neglected. It's cognitively harder to monitor a system passively for errors than to stay engaged in active control. The deskilling effect is real: surgeons using robotic assistants perform fewer manual operations; drivers using adaptive cruise control react slower when manual override is needed. The irony is stark—*systems designed to reduce human error may increase it by diminishing human readiness.*

Moreover, responsibility in autonomous systems is often *proceduralised* rather than personalised. That is, it's embedded in processes and compliance frameworks rather than anchored to moral agents. This creates a culture where following protocol becomes the primary ethical barometer, even if the outcomes are unjust or harmful. Consider the case of predictive policing algorithms, which flag certain neighbourhoods for increased patrol based on historical crime data. Officers may justify biased enforcement by citing algorithmic output. But this deflects moral responsibility away from the lived realities on the street toward the abstract authority of a model—a model whose training data may itself be the residue of past discrimination.

At the heart of this drift is a troubling conceptual shift: from *deciding* to *accepting*. Humans are increasingly positioned not as arbiters but as approvers of algorithmic suggestions. This undermines not just accountability but agency. If the machine said so, then what is left to question? The psychological offloading of responsibility becomes as much a feature of the system as the code itself. And as responsibility becomes harder to locate, so does the motivation to intervene.

One response to this dilemma is transparency. If people better understand how autonomous systems function, perhaps they'll exercise more oversight. Yet transparency is not a panacea. Most AI systems operate on models too complex for even their creators to fully explain. "Black box" neural networks, in particular, defy easy interpretation. Efforts to produce "explainable AI" remain in early stages. And even where explanations are offered, they often come in the form of confidence scores or decision trees that require expert literacy to interpret meaningfully. Transparency without *comprehensibility* does little to restore human control.

Another response is governance: designing institutions that assign responsibility explicitly across the lifecycle of automated systems. This means not just regulating output (e.g., fines for accidents) but embedding responsibility into design decisions, data sourcing, testing protocols, deployment thresholds, and post-deployment audits. Accountability must become a first-order concern, not a downstream legal fix. That means rethinking procurement contracts, liability insurance, and even professional ethics standards for developers and engineers. A failure in an autonomous vehicle or AI diagnostic tool should not simply be a "product defect"—it must be understood as a failure of human foresight, institutional structure, and ethical vigilance.

There is also a cultural challenge: resisting the myth of technological inevitability. Not all automation is progress, and not all delegation is wise. The assumption that every decision can or should be optimised through computation must be interrogated. Systems that operate autonomously may still reflect deeply human choices—what counts as risk, what values are prioritised, who gets to define success. When machines act, they act on human-designed terms. The more we forget this, the more we risk allowing power to hide behind complexity.

Ultimately, *accountability in autonomous systems is not just a question of law—it is a question of civic architecture*. How do we build a society in which technological delegation enhances rather than erodes human responsibility? The answer is not simple, but it is urgent. As more of life is governed by systems no one directly controls, we must resist the temptation to treat harm as a statistical inevitability or moral grey zone. Accountability must be more than a retroactive search for fault. It must be a proactive commitment to foresight, reflection, and answerability—built into the very infrastructure of automation itself.

Chapter 6
Systems of Belief

When a message comes from a machine, we tend to assume it is impartial. That trust—so pervasive, instinctive, and rarely questioned—may be the defining vulnerability of our digital era. Search engines rank results, social feeds curate content, navigation apps chart our course, and most of us assume neutrality. We seldom interrogate the hidden premises on which these outputs rest. Yet every algorithm carries a worldview: decisions about relevance, authority, similarity, and value. These are not merely influencing what we see—they quietly shape what we take to be true.

Digital architectures—search engines, recommendation systems, feedback loops, filters—function as a kind of epistemological scaffolding. They do more than distribute information; they structure the conditions under which knowledge appears credible. When Google surfaces a top result, or TikTok serves a trending clip, the position itself signals authority. Where content appears, how it is framed, often substitutes for critical evaluation. Visibility becomes a proxy for legitimacy. And a pernicious loop emerges: the more something is surfaced, the more it is trusted; the more it is trusted, the more it is surfaced. Belief becomes a function of design rather than deliberation.

The mechanics of predictive text illustrate this subtle influence. Begin typing a query, and your search engine anticipates the rest. Most users select the first suggestion, rarely appreciating that it is shaped not by objective merit but by aggregated behaviours, commercial incentives, and proprietary algorithms. In that instant, agency yields to approximation. Searching becomes guided, curiosity subtly sculpted by the system's expectations.

What renders this epistemic outsourcing so insidious is its seamlessness. Interfaces are designed for ease, speed, and convenience—values few would contest. Yet frictionlessness comes at the cost of reflection. To choose is to weigh; to scroll is to accept. Digital design discourages pause. Platforms pre-empt our preferences, suggest what to watch next, and rank news by engagement metrics—not merely offering options but constructing hierarchies of belief. Unlike traditional newspapers, which make explicit editorial choices, these invisible editors present the world as most clickable, not as it is.

Metrics compound this effect. Ratings, likes, shares, upvotes, follower counts—numerical proxies for credibility—carry an authority that is often misplaced. Five-star reviews may be bot-generated. Viral stories may thrive on outrage rather than substance. Engagement confers legitimacy, not accuracy. Quantification, long associated with rigour, becomes a persuasive device, yet numbers alone mislead. Their authority is contextual, manipulable, cumulative.

The concern is not merely vulnerability to manipulation; it is the colonisation of our understanding of truth. Believing that visibility equals validity, popularity equals insight, or that platforms are impartial conduits, creates a new epistemic fragility. We outsource not only our preferences but our very standards of discernment. When these influence mechanisms are embedded in the tools we use to perceive the world, belief becomes infrastructural.

Social media illustrates this most vividly. Platforms shape identity as much as they reflect it. Users' feeds are filtered not by the diversity of human experience but by optimisation models prioritising engagement. Personalisation becomes a personalised reality: two users searching the same topic may receive radically different information. What is surfaced reinforces prior behaviour rather than challenging it. This insulation shields not only from other perspectives but from the potential for self-transformation.

Technology promised liberation from bias, yet bias persists—reformatted rather than eradicated. In place of overt ideology lies the subtle ideology of "neutral" design: the assumption that unannounced values equate to impartiality. Every system encodes assumptions—about relevance, importance, and success. The illusion of neutrality is maintained through opacity. The less we comprehend the mechanisms, the more we accept outcomes as inevitable.

This is not to portray technology as inherently malign. Digital systems can expand access, reveal injustice, and connect communities. Yet possibility must not be conflated with neutrality. Platforms can amplify dissent while simultaneously burying it; they can promote fact-checks while privileging conspiracy. Infrastructure is never apolitical—it embodies power, and power must be scrutinised.

Systems shape not only what we think but how we think. They mould attention, structure choices, and shape reading habits. A person raised on hyperlinks skims. A student guided by autocomplete accepts prompts. A reader trusting trending topics may cease to question what made them trend. These are epistemological shifts, redefining knowing, believing, and the act of persuasion itself.

This chapter examines how technical systems function as belief systems, how design, data, and digital architecture reinforce dominant norms under the guise of neutrality. We will interrogate the algorithmic aura of truth, the persuasive authority of metrics, and the subtle ways interface design directs cognition. Most crucially, we will ask how to resist this drift: how to remain epistemically vigilant in an environment optimised for passivity. The stakes are not abstract. In a world mediated by machines, understanding belief is inseparable from understanding infrastructure. Failing to see the systems shaping our convictions risks mistaking convenience for comprehension—and influence for insight.

Infrastructure Shapes Ideology

The power of an idea is often mistaken for its inherent truth, when in fact it may simply be the product of repeated exposure, selective amplification, and design defaults. The systems we interact with daily—search engines, navigation apps, news feeds, recommendation engines—do not merely distribute information. They structure the experience of reality itself. Beneath their surface efficiencies lies a deeper function: the quiet shaping of norms, assumptions, and beliefs that feel natural not because they are true, but because the infrastructure makes them so.

What makes infrastructure ideologically potent is precisely its invisibility. No one looks at a bridge and sees a worldview, yet every piece of infrastructure encodes decisions about who gets to move where, when, and how. In the digital realm, that logic is magnified. Consider the simple act of searching. A user enters a query into Google and receives ranked results. The interface suggests objectivity, efficiency, even neutrality. But those rankings are shaped by algorithms optimised for engagement, historical click patterns, searcher profiles, and advertiser bids. The system privileges certain sources, suppresses others, and ranks what is presumed most relevant—without explaining on what grounds. Over time, this shapes a habit: trust the top result. What was originally a design choice becomes a cognitive reflex. *Infrastructure becomes ideology by becoming habit.*

Take the example of Facebook's News Feed, once lauded as a personal newspaper tailored to each user's interests. But "interest" is a misleading term. What appears in the feed is not determined by expressed intention but by measured behaviour: what the user clicked, hovered over, liked, or shared in the past. The algorithm then delivers more of the same. What looks like personalisation is actually reinforcement. The ideology embedded here is subtle but consequential—*past engagement determines future visibility.* And so, over time, the user's informational environment becomes less diverse, more emotionally charged, and increasingly self-confirming. The system appears to serve the individual, but in reality it disciplines the mind. It rewards repetition over exploration, reaction over reflection.

These examples are not isolated glitches but central features of how modern platforms operate. Designers optimise for efficiency, growth, and engagement. But each of these objectives requires choices: What counts as a meaningful action? What kind of behaviour should be encouraged? What content deserves visibility? These are not technical questions. They are moral and cultural decisions cloaked in mathematical language. When the outputs of such systems are accepted as neutral—because they are automated, quantified, and fast—they begin to displace other ways of knowing. *What cannot be measured becomes what cannot be seen.*

This is how dominant ideologies perpetuate themselves in digital systems—not through overt coercion, but through architectural defaults. If a ride-sharing app refuses to serve areas with low historical demand, it quietly encodes class and racial bias into its logistics. If a credit-scoring algorithm penalises applicants from less-documented financial backgrounds, it embeds historical inequality into future access. If image-recognition systems are trained predominantly on Western faces, their errors will disproportionately affect those who don't conform. In each case, the system's logic appears impartial. But the outcomes reflect inherited biases, silently magnified by scale.

Even something as seemingly benign as a "trending" list reveals the ideological nature of infrastructure. What becomes trending is not simply what is popular, but what the system determines to be accelerating in attention. That determination is based on rate-of-change metrics, not absolute volume, and is subject to internal thresholds that are rarely made public. This creates a distorted mirror of public interest—some topics are amplified prematurely, others are buried despite wide relevance. And because "trending" is perceived as an indicator of importance, it shapes the very interest it reports. The platform tells the user what to pay attention to, and the user, trusting the platform, complies. *A feedback loop forms between infrastructure and belief.*

Contrast this with earlier systems of knowledge organisation—libraries, broadcast media, academic publishing. Each had its own biases and hierarchies, but they also had traceable editorial processes, standards of evidence, and institutional accountability. Digital infrastructure replaces that logic with opaque automation. The editors are now algorithms. The standards are click-through rates. The accountability mechanisms are reactive, not structural. When users encounter misinformation, harassment, or systemic bias, the response is often to "improve the algorithm." But what if the problem is not a broken tool, but the very assumption that the tool can ever be neutral?

The claim to neutrality is not incidental. It is central to the ideology of technical systems. Engineers often speak of "scaling" solutions, "removing friction," and "empowering users." But these goals presume that the system is a passive facilitator rather than an active participant. They obscure the fact that every system encodes values: what kind of interaction is encouraged, what kind of user is imagined, what kind of future is anticipated. A navigation app that always routes the shortest path assumes that speed is the overriding priority. A job platform that ranks candidates by keyword matches assumes that qualifications can be inferred from textual similarity. A dating app that sorts profiles based on swipe history assumes that desire is a function of past behaviour. Each of these assumptions may be defensible. But they are not value-free. They are *normative choices embedded in technical design*.

One might argue that infrastructure merely reflects the world rather than shapes it. But reflection is never perfect. It is selective, biased, and recursive. The more a system reflects what it sees, the more it reifies what it reflects. If the world is unequal, and the system amplifies patterns of inequality under the guise of relevance, then the infrastructure is not merely descriptive—it is constitutive. It builds the future by reinforcing the past. In doing so, it shifts the burden of scrutiny from designers to users, from systems to individuals. This absolves the infrastructure of responsibility, even as it becomes the dominant medium of influence.

To resist this drift, one must develop *infrastructural literacy*—the ability to see systems not as neutral conduits, but as sites of contestation. This means asking hard questions: Who designed this system? What assumptions guided its architecture? Whose interests are served? Whose voices are missing? What alternatives were ignored? It also means demanding transparency, accountability, and pluralism—not just in content, but in the underlying logic of the platforms we rely on. *Ideological neutrality is not a feature of infrastructure; it is a myth sustained by opacity.*

The stakes are not just technical. They are philosophical and political. When belief is shaped by infrastructure, and infrastructure is governed by private interests, the boundary between influence and control becomes dangerously thin. The more we accept systems as inevitable, the less we question their design. The more we trust automation, the less we invest in critical thinking. And the more we rely on platforms to mediate our reality, the more they define what that reality is allowed to be.

Ultimately, infrastructure is never just about function. It is about *framing*. It tells us what matters, who counts, how to navigate, and what to believe. When these frames are invisible, their power increases. To see them clearly is the first step toward reclaiming agency—not just over our tools, but over the ideologies they silently enforce.

The Algorithmic Aura of Truth

When a query is typed into a search bar, what unfolds in response often feels less like a suggestion and more like a verdict. The top result appears not merely relevant but definitive, imbued with a kind of epistemic authority that transcends its source. This deference to algorithmic output is one of the most consequential epistemological shifts of our time. It marks a transition from human mediation to machinic arbitration in the hierarchy of knowledge, where *who says something* matters less than *where it ranks*. This is the *algorithmic aura of truth*—the widespread belief that the output of a system is more reliable than the motivations of its authors.

This phenomenon is neither accidental nor superficial. It is the product of cultural, technological, and psychological factors that have converged to make algorithmic systems appear objective, impartial, and precise. Trust in algorithms often exceeds trust in institutions, media outlets, or academic expertise—not because users have analysed the code or verified its fairness, but because the interface conceals complexity behind seamless design. *The cleaner the output, the deeper the trust.* When results arrive quickly, consistently, and without visible bias, users interpret this speed and coherence as a sign of accuracy. The architecture of modern platforms capitalises on this perception, making algorithms appear like omniscient arbiters rather than fallible tools shaped by human agendas.

At the heart of this dynamic is a fundamental inversion of the evidentiary process. In traditional epistemology, the credibility of an assertion depends on the source's authority, context, and rationale. In the digital context, the visibility of an assertion becomes its warrant. A trending hashtag, a top-ranked search result, a recommended video—all derive their perceived legitimacy from their position within a system, not from the robustness of their argument. *Prominence becomes a proxy for truth.* The user rarely asks why something is trending or why it appears first; they simply infer that it must matter.

Consider the way YouTube's recommendation engine operates. A user watches a video on climate science and is immediately served a cascade of related content. Over time, the system refines its predictions, favouring videos that produce longer watch times and higher engagement. But engagement is a poor proxy for epistemic value. A sensationalised or misleading video may outperform a rigorous, nuanced one. Yet the algorithm, agnostic to truth and sensitive only to performance metrics, elevates the former. The user, unaware of this logic, interprets visibility as endorsement. In this way, *systems designed for relevance become engines of belief,* shaping not only what people see but how they understand what they see.

What makes the algorithmic aura of truth so insidious is its *interface of neutrality*. Unlike a human editor who might disclose their political leaning or cite editorial policy, an algorithm presents itself as neutral. Its authority is derived not from persuasion but from perceived impartiality. Google's minimalist interface, for instance, offers no editorial commentary—only a ranked list. This design suggests that the answers speak for themselves. In reality, every aspect of that list is shaped by choices: which signals to weight, how to interpret relevance, what kinds of content to penalise or boost. These are deeply consequential decisions, yet they are obscured by a veneer of objectivity.

This is not merely a matter of design ethics. It has profound consequences for democratic discourse, scientific understanding, and social cohesion. When algorithmic rankings determine what is seen and what is buried, they structure the conditions under which public reasoning occurs. Take the example of political information on social media. Posts that provoke outrage or strong emotional reactions tend to be shared more widely, and thus are promoted by algorithms optimised for engagement. This means that the visibility of a political claim often reflects its affective intensity, not its factual accuracy. Yet users interpret the claim's popularity as indicative of its legitimacy. *Emotion-driven amplification masquerades as consensus.*

The trust placed in algorithmic outputs is further reinforced by the feedback loops they generate. Once a piece of content gains visibility, it attracts more clicks, which reinforces its rank, which draws more clicks still. This recursive dynamic creates self-validating hierarchies of information. The system doesn't merely reflect interest—it manufactures it. Users encountering this content at the top of their feed or results page assume that it reflects broad public consensus, when in fact it may be the product of an initial spike in attention that was algorithmically magnified. *The algorithm does not find the truth; it constructs its visibility.*

Moreover, the aura of truth surrounding algorithmic outputs is intensified by the erosion of traditional gatekeepers. Newspapers, universities, and encyclopedias once served as arbiters of accuracy, albeit imperfectly. Their authority rested on institutional norms, editorial oversight, and professional codes. Today, these signals are drowned in the noise of decentralised platforms, where all content competes on the same aesthetic and structural terms. A video from a peer-reviewed medical journal and one from a conspiracy theorist may appear side-by-side in a user's recommendations. If the platform presents both as equally clickable, and the user lacks contextual knowledge, the line between information and misinformation blurs. *Platform design flattens epistemic distinctions.*

This does not mean that algorithms are intrinsically deceptive or that users are irrational. Rather, it points to a deeper structural problem: *a mismatch between the epistemic demands of a pluralistic society and the optimisation logics of digital platforms*. The systems that curate our information flows are designed to maximise attention, not understanding. They are engineered for stickiness, not scrutiny. And yet we lean on them to make decisions about health, politics, history, and ethics. This gap between purpose and perception is where the aura of truth thrives.

A particularly revealing case is that of predictive text systems in search engines. When a user begins typing a query, autocomplete suggestions appear—often reflecting the most common searches made by others. These suggestions feel like guidance, and their placement near the input field implies authority. But what they actually represent is statistical frequency. The system is not saying "this is the right question to ask" but "this is what others tend to type next." Yet many users take these prompts as meaningful hints, even endorsements. *Statistical patterns become epistemic cues,* not because they are logical, but because they are presented with immediacy and fluency.

The psychological underpinning of this trust is known as *automation bias*—the tendency to favour suggestions made by automated systems, even when they contradict human judgment. In high-stakes domains such as healthcare, aviation, or criminal justice, automation bias can have serious consequences. A radiologist may overlook a tumour because the AI system didn't flag it. A judge may over-rely on a risk score without questioning its basis. In these contexts, the aura of algorithmic truth does not merely mislead—it governs action. *The appearance of objectivity becomes a substitute for accountability.*

To challenge the algorithmic aura of truth, it is not enough to demand better algorithms. What is needed is a cultural shift in how we interpret and relate to system-generated outputs. This begins with recognising that all algorithms are *instruments of interpretation,* not revelation. Their outputs are artefacts of design choices, data biases, and optimisation goals. They should be interrogated, contextualised, and—when necessary—resisted. This requires both technical transparency and *epistemic humility*: an awareness that no output, however seamless, should escape scrutiny simply because it came from a machine.

The broader imperative is to foster systems that prioritise *epistemic integrity* over engagement efficiency. This might mean incorporating deliberative friction—slowing down the user to consider source credibility before sharing. It might involve clearer metadata about content provenance, algorithmic rationales, or editorial standards. It might require pluralistic ranking systems that surface diverse viewpoints rather than converging on consensus. But above all, it requires reasserting human judgment at the centre of knowledge-making. *The machine may assist, but it must not replace discernment.*

The challenge of the algorithmic age is not that people have lost the ability to think critically, but that the infrastructure of their digital environment increasingly shapes what is seen, what is believed, and what is trusted. The aura of truth around algorithmic outputs is a cultural artefact—built by design, reinforced by habit, and sustained by opacity. Disarming it begins with naming it, and with building alternatives that reward not just what captures attention, but what withstands examination.

Quantified Authority

A 4.8-star restaurant on a review app appears trustworthy, not merely appetising. A university ranked "Top 10" globally is assumed to be inherently superior. A person with 500,000 followers is treated as a thought leader before they say a word. Across digital life, numbers have become the most persuasive form of authority—not because they are necessarily correct, but because they appear *unassailable*. *Quantification does not just summarise status; it confers it.* In digital systems where complexity is collapsed into simple scores, the very act of being counted becomes a credential. The result is a world governed by metrics—elegant in appearance, yet often flawed, skewed, or fundamentally misleading.

The illusion of precision is powerful. Platforms routinely collapse multidimensional qualities into single indicators—stars, likes, follower counts, or rankings—creating a veneer of objectivity. These figures carry an air of neutrality, as if they exist outside of human bias or institutional interests. In practice, however, *metrics are not discovered; they are designed*. The decision to measure engagement over nuance, click-throughs over comprehension, or velocity over depth is a choice, not a natural law. These choices encode incentives that shape not just what gets seen, but what gets made. *Quantified authority is not passive—it directs culture.*

Consider the architecture of rating systems on e-commerce platforms. A product with thousands of positive reviews rises in search visibility and consumer confidence, while a newer or niche item struggles to break through. The numerical advantage reinforces itself in a cycle of visibility, purchase, and further review accumulation. But beneath this feedback loop lies a deeply fragile signal. Reviews can be gamed through bots or incentivised responses. Negative experiences are often underreported due to social desirability bias or friction in the complaint process. Yet the composite score remains unchallenged, treated as a stable truth. *What appears democratic is often driven by noise, not insight.*

This trust in quantification extends well beyond consumer products. In the academic world, journal impact factors influence funding and promotion decisions, despite being a poor proxy for article quality. In the creative economy, content creators are judged by subscriber counts, not by the intellectual rigour or originality of their output. In journalism, article headlines are A/B tested for click performance, which then feeds into algorithmic promotion. These numbers are treated as performance metrics, but they often become identity markers—recasting *who someone is* in terms of *how they score*. The result is an epistemic environment where being well-ranked trumps being well-reasoned.

Nowhere is this dynamic more acute than in search engine results. Google's page ranking algorithm is an archetype of quantified authority—elevating content based on hundreds of weighted factors, many of which relate to popularity, backlink volume, or user interaction. The user sees only a clean, ordered list. They rarely question the criteria or consider what is excluded. Yet this ranking is not an index of truth, but a complex prediction of what users are likely to click. *The map is not the territory, but it is treated as gospel.* This matters because search results are not just answers—they are endorsements. Being in the top spot *is* being authoritative, whether the underlying content earns that position or not.

The danger lies not in quantification per se, but in the conflation of numerical representation with epistemic reliability. A number feels final. It short-circuits deliberation. A 5-star Uber driver is "safe," a 3.7-star Airbnb is "fine," a 2.4-star book is "not worth reading." Yet the numerical summary conceals everything that cannot be standardised: context, expectation, cultural variation, and interpersonal complexity. The review may reflect frustration with the weather, not the service; the rating may come from one demographic but apply to all. Still, the system encourages us to treat the number as definitive. *Numbers feel like facts, even when they are artefacts.*

This is compounded by interface design that *amplifies metric salience*. The number of likes is shown prominently, reinforcing its relevance. Scores are colour-coded to guide perception. "Top rated" badges are visually distinct, lending further gravitas. The interface does not just present the metric; it *curates* the user's attention toward it. This design logic is rarely questioned because it feels frictionless. But the friction removed is the cognitive kind—the kind that asks, "Should I trust this number? Should I probe further?" *Frictionless trust is expedient, but often intellectually lazy.*

Philosophically, quantified authority rests on a positivist illusion: that knowledge is more valid the more it can be measured. But many domains of human experience resist neat quantification. Consider the evaluation of a therapist, a novel, or a teaching experience. Each contains intangible dimensions—empathy, creativity, intellectual resonance—that defy star ratings. When systems attempt to reduce these to numbers, they strip away complexity in favour of legibility. *What cannot be measured becomes invisible.* And what is visible becomes overvalued.

This logic also infiltrates institutional decisions. University league tables, often derived from dubious weighting of disparate variables, drive student enrolment and funding. Police departments are evaluated by arrest quotas or response times, which can distort priorities and encourage manipulative practices. Hospitals may be rated on readmission rates, prompting behaviours that avoid high-risk patients rather than improve care. *Metrics can incentivise what they claim to evaluate, distorting the very reality they aim to reflect.*

Moreover, once metrics become embedded in reputation systems, they acquire a *moral dimension*. A low score becomes a sign of failure, not just performance. A content creator with fewer followers is seen as less credible. A restaurant with mixed reviews is presumed careless. These judgments feed into career trajectories, business outcomes, and public perception. *Quantification becomes a social sorting mechanism*—efficient, scalable, and devastatingly reductive.

To challenge this hegemony of the metric, one must first recognise its cultural allure. Numbers appear impartial in an age of polarisation. They offer certainty in a context of overload. They promise fairness without friction. But they do so by eliding ambiguity, context, and dissent. The task, then, is not to abandon measurement, but to *reframe its meaning*. A rating should be a starting point for inquiry, not the endpoint of judgment. A ranking should prompt curiosity about its criteria, not obedience to its order.

There are alternatives. Systems can foreground qualitative data—actual review content—rather than burying it beneath an aggregate score. Platforms can offer transparency about how metrics are generated and allow users to filter by criteria they value. Decision-making environments can prioritise deliberation over reaction, encouraging users to consider nuance before endorsing or rejecting. *The goal is not anti-metric, but post-metric*: a shift from passive consumption of quantified output to active interrogation of what those numbers represent.

Quantified authority thrives because it feels easy. It resolves complexity into order. But it is precisely in the *unresolved* space—between numbers, beneath rankings, behind scores—that real discernment begins. To see numbers not as truths, but as tools, is to reclaim the authority we have too quickly outsourced. Authority, after all, should rest not in the number, but in the mind interpreting it.

Belief by Design

Every interface teaches. Whether it intends to or not, the structure of a digital environment nudges, narrows, or expands how people come to understand the world. Scroll through a news app, and you'll notice which stories appear at the top and which fade into obscurity. Search for a topic on a video platform, and you'll be guided not just by the first result, but by the visual cues—thumbnail, duration, comments—that subtly shape what feels trustworthy or worth watching. None of these design decisions are neutral. *The architecture of information is the architecture of belief.*

Design, in its purest form, is a language—visual, spatial, interactive. But when that language is deployed in systems that mediate truth claims, political discourse, scientific understanding, or moral debate, it becomes more than functional. It becomes ideological. The design of menus, notification systems, and content feeds doesn't just help users navigate an interface—it helps structure their assumptions about what matters, what is normal, what is credible, and what should be ignored. *Belief is not merely argued into existence; it is scaffolded into being by repeated patterns of exposure and attention.*

Consider the search box—ubiquitous, innocuous, and powerful. A user types in a query, and the platform suggests auto-completions. These suggestions, drawn from popularity or past behaviour, not only reflect but also amplify collective sentiment. A query that begins "Why are immigrants…" might yield radically different options based on prevailing user inputs—some benign, some laced with prejudice. The user, seeing a drop-down menu of options, interprets these not just as data, but as evidence of societal consensus. *The autocomplete isn't just predictive—it's persuasive.*

This extends to feed-based environments, where content architecture determines the order, prominence, and frequency of exposure. On platforms like TikTok or Instagram, where algorithmic discovery replaces social curation, the belief-shaping work of the interface intensifies. The user is not merely selecting what to consume; they are being shown what to want. Popularity begets visibility, visibility begets trust, and trust becomes belief. This is not manipulation in the overt sense; it's something subtler and more enduring—a *systemic shaping of thought via exposure mechanics.*

One of the most profound shifts in the digital era is the inversion of intentionality. People no longer seek information as much as information seeks them. In this context, interface design plays the role of gatekeeper. What is surfaced on a homepage, what is tucked behind a hamburger menu, what is framed as "breaking" or "recommended"—these are not trivial editorial choices. They are acts of epistemological framing. If news about climate change is buried beneath sports and celebrity gossip, the user learns implicitly that ecological urgency is marginal. *Design orders priority, and priority shapes perception.*

Design decisions also shape *how* belief is formed. A platform that foregrounds user comments can reinforce the impression that knowledge is democratically constructed. One that suppresses comment visibility fosters an air of institutional authority. Similarly, reactions—likes, hearts, retweets—become social validators, signalling what others value. But these signals are themselves curated. Platforms may weight reactions differently, promote some forms of engagement over others, or reset counters based on backend adjustments. The result is a perception of consensus that is engineered, not emergent. *The crowd becomes a tool of influence, not an independent check.*

Even the visual design of content—fonts, colours, hierarchy—plays a role in credibility. Research in information literacy has shown that users often trust aesthetically polished websites over those that appear amateurish, regardless of factual accuracy. This gives sophisticated propagandists an advantage and penalises underfunded but rigorous sources. It also means that design fluency becomes a proxy for epistemic reliability. If it looks professional, it *feels* true. *This aesthetic conflation of polish with truth is one of the quietest yet most pervasive distortions in the belief landscape.*

Philosophically, the issue traces back to Marshall McLuhan's dictum: *the medium is the message*. But in today's ecosystem, the *interface* is the medium, and its message is infrastructural. It's not just what you say, but how and where it's displayed that determines its effect. Belief does not arise in a vacuum; it crystallises in environments designed to optimise attention, minimise friction, and maximise user retention. In such settings, design isn't a backdrop—it's the stage manager, scriptwriter, and sometimes even the main character.

Yet it's not only persuasion that occurs through design—it's resistance, too. Users can and do challenge design-led narratives, often by modding systems, creating counter-interfaces, or engaging in critical literacy. Browser extensions that re-order Twitter feeds chronologically rather than algorithmically are one example. Platforms like Reddit, where users control upvote mechanics more directly, represent a different model of visibility. Still, even in these cases, the foundational architecture limits what can be contested. *You can resist within the frame, but rarely outside it.*

Educational systems have not caught up. Digital literacy curriculums tend to focus on evaluating content—checking sources, spotting fake news—while neglecting the deeper layer: *evaluating the design of the system itself.* This oversight leaves users vulnerable to what scholars call *interface determinism*—the uncritical assumption that the design of a platform reflects some optimal or neutral order. When users fail to interrogate why a platform presents information as it does, they surrender interpretive agency. They read the interface as a mirror, not a map drawn with intent.

This matters not just for personal belief, but for public discourse. Democracies rely on a shared epistemic foundation—some sense of what is knowable, debatable, or settled. When belief formation is silently stratified by divergent design systems—each with its own logics of amplification, exclusion, and aesthetic coding—that foundation fractures. *Design becomes destiny*, and collective sense-making becomes harder to achieve. The most dangerous epistemic divide may not be between left and right, or expert and layperson, but between those who see interfaces as epistemological actors and those who do not.

So what can be done? Designers bear responsibility—not for controlling belief, but for creating systems that *disclose their own logics*. Transparency about ranking mechanisms, customisation options for feed structures, and friction layers that encourage reflection are all promising directions. More radically, users could be given *design agency*—the ability to tailor their own attention environments beyond superficial themes or dark mode toggles. *Design should not only be experienced; it should be understood, questioned, and, when necessary, redesigned.*

Belief by design is not an anomaly. It is the new normal. In a world where every click is a decision and every layout a proposition, belief is no longer simply inherited, argued, or taught. It is *interfaced*. The question is not whether design shapes belief, but whether we can learn to shape design in ways that preserve intellectual autonomy, epistemic humility, and the messy, vital plurality of thought. To do so is not just to use digital systems—but to understand them as belief systems in their own right.

Chapter 7
The Platformed Self

To exist online is to be visible. Yet in the attention-driven economies of digital platforms, visibility is never neutral—it is shaping. The social self, once a delicate balance of private reflection, public performance, and interpersonal nuance, is now entwined with algorithmic logic. Every scroll, like, and click becomes a traceable signal, measured, compared, and endlessly refined. In such an environment, identity is less a personal narrative than a perpetually updated data construct. We are no longer merely users; we are curated products—algorithmically optimised for engagement and prominence.

This transformation is deliberate and enduring. Platforms operate on profiling logics that far exceed simple demographic segmentation. They construct psychographic projections, composite portraits informed by your Spotify playlists, late-night searches, and even the timing of your interactions. These are not passive archives of behaviour; they actively shape the content you see, the advertisements you encounter, and the responses you elicit from others. Identity, once expressed, is now anticipated.

What begins as convenience soon slides into distortion. Search once for a parenting article, and your feed quickly floods with nappies, behavioural tips, and toys. The platform has made a judgement, and your data trail reinforces it. Friends and family, observing your posts and likes, unconsciously adjust their perception of you. Your digital persona accrues gravity—not necessarily in alignment with your intentions, yet increasingly constraining your expression. Divergence grows harder; your profile becomes a lens through which both you and others perceive you.

At the same time, users consciously navigate this terrain. Many, through intuition or trial and error, learn which expressions attract attention. Vulnerable tweets garner retweets; subtle arguments may go unnoticed. Platform literacy becomes performative fluency. People no longer post merely what they think—they post what performs. The reward mechanisms of digital platforms shape not only expression but thought itself, subtly altering what is felt worth articulating.

Agency exists, but it is bounded. Users are neither blank slates nor helpless victims; they curate images, manage tone, and time posts with sophistication. Yet this agency is situated: it unfolds within systems engineered for continuous behavioural capture. The algorithm reflects not just what you are, but what you were rewarded for being. It remembers; it predicts.

Feedback loops intensify this entanglement. Post a gym selfie, receive likes, and your fitness identity strengthens. Watch political videos, and the platform nudges you further down an ideological corridor. You begin to anticipate your audience's response, calibrating offline behaviour to match the online persona that is already "performing." This is not simply self versus audience; it is self observing self, mediated through machine.

Psychological and social consequences follow. Scholars of "context collapse" note how platforms compress distinct social spheres: your boss, a cousin, a stranger abroad—all witness the same post, yet interpret it differently. Authenticity becomes risky; ambiguity dangerous. Users optimise for clarity, humour, or outrage. Expression narrows; identity narrows with it.

This is not only performance. Platforms instantiate identity. A dating app bio, an Instagram archive, an Amazon history—these extend beyond representation into active self-construction. Choices are recorded, shaped, and anticipated, producing interoperable data states that are portable, platform-specific, and subject to reclassification.

Social dynamics are similarly reframed. Friendships and affinities are filtered through algorithmic suggestion. Who is recommended, who appears in your feed, who gains visibility? Platforms now structure not just what we see, but who sees us—and on what terms. Visibility itself becomes a form of social and epistemic capital. Unseen, one risks erasure.

These pressures are not evenly distributed. Marginalised users face intensified labour: code-switching, managing exposure, navigating moderation. Authenticity can invite harassment; conformity offers protection. Identity becomes both curated and defended. Online selfhood is a constant calculation of cost.

Generational differences are apparent. Digital natives, raised amidst perpetual visibility, often integrate online and offline selves seamlessly. For them, platforms are not appendages to identity—they are formative. Their preferences, aesthetics, and relational styles emerge within these architectures, rather than being retrofitted onto them.

Where, then, does agency reside? Every act of expression is framed, filtered, and rewarded within opaque systems. Yet agency does not vanish; it mutates. It is iterative, situational, paradoxical. Users can be complicit and subversive simultaneously. A TikTok creator may parody influencer culture while exploiting its tropes. A Twitter user may critique platform capitalism even as they amplify their own profile. Reflexivity becomes literacy.

Still, reflexivity has limits. Awareness does not confer immunity. Knowing one is shaped does not dissolve the shaping. True reclamation may demand more than self-conscious strategy. It may require infrastructures that prioritise transparency, plurality, and friction—spaces where identity can breathe without needing to perform.

The stakes extend beyond authenticity to the very nature of personhood. Identities, now data products subject to commodification, surveillance, and algorithmic refinement, raise urgent questions: who decides what we are? In platform societies, this is no abstraction. It is an operational system, running millions of times per second. Selfhood has become computable—and, in consequence, contestable.

The platformed self is not a temporary anomaly; it is a reconfiguration of the conditions of identity itself. To grasp this is to confront the machinery beneath daily expression, and to ask—sometimes quietly, sometimes urgently—what kinds of selves these systems are teaching us to become.

Identity as a Data Product

Identity has always been partly performative. From the clothes we wear to the company we keep, humans have long curated aspects of themselves for social acceptance, protection, or influence. But never before has identity been *engineered* by external systems to the extent it is today. In the architecture of digital platforms, selfhood is no longer just expressed—it is *calculated*. Constructed through the debris of clicks, likes, searches, and scrolls, identity becomes a *data product*: a dynamic, probabilistic representation continuously refined by machine learning models and deployed for behavioural prediction and monetisation. This profile is not merely used to recommend ads or content; it shapes the very lenses through which others see and respond to us—and through which we come to see ourselves.

Contrary to the belief that social media simply offers us a louder megaphone or a broader canvas for self-expression, the more consequential shift is one of authorship. *We are no longer the sole authors of our own identities.* Platforms like Facebook, TikTok, Instagram, and LinkedIn do not merely host our expressions; they interpret, sort, and rank them. More significantly, they recombine signals we never explicitly offered—location history, device usage, dwell time, browsing behaviour—into profiles that exceed our conscious self-presentation. This inferred self then becomes the operative version: the "you" advertisers target, the "you" that algorithmic feeds tailor, the "you" whose preferences are extrapolated, and the "you" who is served to others in search results or friend suggestions. In effect, *your identity becomes a product consumed by systems and others before it is even fully known to you.*

This process is obscured by a veneer of personalisation. It feels as if the feed knows you intimately, when in fact it knows only a mathematically derived abstraction of you. And yet, because its recommendations are responsive and often effective, we come to trust its reflection. *When the algorithm seems to understand us better than we understand ourselves, it is tempting to believe that what it shows us is who we are.* This is the quiet epistemic shift: from being the narrator of one's story to being the subject of a behavioural prediction model.

The datafication of identity has consequences that extend beyond personal branding or ad targeting. It reshapes social perception in granular and often invisible ways. Consider a dating app like Hinge. Your profile may include photos, prompts, and preferences, but the platform's behavioural model also considers your swipes, reply times, message content, and profile edits. It calculates a desirability score and silently adjusts your visibility accordingly. You may be unaware of how often you're shown to others—or why. The model's decisions, however, affect how often you're matched, how others interpret your desirability, and even how you come to assess your own attractiveness or worth. The same logic applies on professional platforms like LinkedIn, where your engagement with industry content may raise your discoverability within certain sectors or determine how recruiters assess your "fit." *The identity others see is filtered through what the platform wants to show them, which is filtered through what it thinks you are good for*.

This filtering is not neutral. It privileges certain traits, behaviours, and identities over others, in ways aligned with platform incentives. People who post frequently, generate engagement, or conform to the platform's aesthetic or ideological norms are rewarded with greater visibility. Conversely, those who resist gamified participation or fall outside normative models are rendered invisible. What looks like popularity is often simply the successful alignment of a user's behaviour with the platform's optimisation objectives. What looks like neglect may be a form of algorithmic exclusion. *Visibility is engineered, not earned.*

The implications for social interaction are subtle but profound. On platforms that simulate public space—Twitter, TikTok, Facebook—identity is *not* a stable self-image projected to a known audience. It is a fluctuating index calculated from ambient data and mediated through opaque systems. When you see someone's post, you are not just seeing their thought—you are seeing what the platform's identity engine has decided is their most performative or monetisable expression. Over time, our impressions of others become less grounded in shared context and more shaped by *machine-curated representations of people*. This erodes not just authenticity, but also relational trust.

Such distortions can also turn inward. As users absorb and internalise the version of themselves reflected back through algorithmic suggestion—what ads target them, what content trends in their feed, what personas earn traction—they may start to align their behaviour with the inferred identity. A user who repeatedly receives fitness ads may begin to see herself primarily through that lens. A person whose posts only gain traction when they express outrage may feel compelled to adopt a more combative tone. This is not simple pandering; it is a form of *algorithmic conditioning*. The system does not dictate who you are, but it *nudges you toward the version of yourself that the system finds most legible and profitable.*

Such identity shaping can be especially consequential in developmental contexts. Teenagers forming their sense of self in real time are subjected to continuous feedback loops—likes, follows, reposts—that act as micro-validations or rejections of particular identities. The impact is not limited to self-esteem; it alters identity formation itself. The incentive to be seen and affirmed in platform logic overrides quieter forms of self-discovery. The self becomes *not something to uncover, but something to market test.*

Not all identity constructions are equally shaped. Racial, gendered, and class-based profiling amplify these effects. Studies have shown that Black users are disproportionately shown ads for lower-paying jobs, that LGBTQ+ identities face higher rates of algorithmic flagging and de-platforming, and that Indigenous profiles are underrepresented in search visibility. These are not isolated glitches; they are emergent properties of systems trained on historical bias and designed for commercial optimisation. *When identity becomes a data product, existing social inequalities are not corrected—they are codified, scaled, and rendered less visible under the guise of objectivity.*

It is tempting to dismiss all this as the price of convenience, or to lean into a narrative of inevitability. But such fatalism concedes too much. The systems that turn identity into product are not laws of nature; they are design choices. Their logics are contestable, their parameters adjustable, and their operations subject to governance. Alternative architectures exist—ones that could centre user agency, preserve identity pluralism, or at the very least, render identity computation legible and accountable. *The issue is not that datafied identity exists, but that we are largely unaware of the extent to which it governs how we are seen, understood, and treated.*

Ultimately, the transformation of identity into a data product invites a reconsideration of the self in digital life. Are we the sum of our behavioural traces, as machines perceive them? Are we what others see, through platform-determined lenses? Or is there still room for selfhood that exceeds computational modelling? These are not theoretical questions. They shape our interpersonal relationships, our employment prospects, our civic participation, and our mental well-being. In a world where identity is increasingly a platform-mediated construct, reclaiming authorship over the self may be one of the most urgent acts of digital resistance.

But resistance begins with recognition. And recognition begins with understanding that the "you" being acted upon—by algorithms, by advertisers, by other users—is not simply *you*. It is a datafied fiction, continuously updated, owned by no one, interpreted by everyone, and designed above all to serve the needs of the system. *The challenge is not to dismantle identity, but to decouple the self from the systems that presume to know it better than we do.*

Performance and Personalisation

To exist on a digital platform today is to perform. Not in the theatrical sense, but in a subtler, algorithmically informed posture: curated, measured, and optimised for visibility. The architecture of social platforms has made identity into a kind of real-time interface—something perpetually adjustable in response to audience reactions and system feedback. As personal expression becomes entwined with content strategy, users are incentivised not simply to be *seen*, but to be *favoured* by machine-driven curation. And favour, in this context, depends not on authenticity but on alignment with patterns that the algorithm recognises, rewards, and amplifies. *The result is an ecosystem in which self-presentation becomes a data-informed performance calibrated to satisfy machines, not just other people.*

Social platforms—whether Instagram, YouTube, TikTok, LinkedIn, or even Goodreads—are not neutral stages. They are environments designed to reward particular patterns of engagement. A platform's feed ranks what content a user sees based on prediction models trained to maximise retention, advertising revenue, or daily active users. This ranking is opaque, yet its effects are legible to anyone who has posted a piece of content that was inexplicably ignored—or suddenly went viral. Over time, patterns emerge. Users observe, implicitly or analytically, what kind of content seems to succeed. Posts that conform to platform-specific aesthetics, timing conventions, sentiment styles, and engagement tactics often perform better. This leads to what some scholars term *algorithmic impression management*: the active tailoring of one's digital persona in response to algorithmic cues rather than personal conviction or social feedback.

Take, for instance, TikTok creators. Success on the platform often hinges on highly specific, often fleeting stylistic tropes—certain camera angles, audio clips, caption formats, or even facial expressions that signal to the system a particular genre or community. The more tightly a video fits these moulds, the more likely it is to be shown to similar audiences, boosting engagement and encouraging further conformity. Creators are aware of this, and many adapt accordingly—modifying not just their content, but their *behavioural rhythms* to match what the system expects. The line between participation and self-modulation begins to blur. *What feels like creativity becomes conditioned replication.*

This is not limited to influencers or content creators. Everyday users engage in similar micro-adjustments. A user on LinkedIn may exaggerate enthusiasm in a post because they've observed that positive, inspirational tones garner more attention. A reader on Goodreads may only post reviews for popular books, having noticed that obscure titles receive little engagement. A Twitter user may craft threads in a style optimised for retweets, even if it feels performative. These adaptations are not inherently dishonest; they reflect a pragmatic understanding of what the system rewards. But when visibility depends on consistency with algorithmic norms, users face a choice: to express oneself fully and risk being ignored, or to align with expectation and be seen. *Personalisation becomes not a service, but a feedback mechanism that quietly governs performance.*

The concept of personalisation—once a selling point for platforms—has subtly redefined agency. It suggests a system that learns about you, adapts to you, understands you. But personalisation is not a mirror; it is a filter. It selects and amplifies content based on past behaviour, then uses your response to that content to further shape what you see. Over time, this creates a kind of *algorithmic tunnel vision* in which the platform shows you only what you have previously engaged with, or what it predicts you might. This creates a recursive loop: you perform in ways the system rewards, and the system rewards you with content that reflects that performance. The self becomes caught in a closed circuit of optimisation.

In this loop, *the boundaries between intention and influence become difficult to trace*. Are you sharing that particular article because you truly care about its subject, or because similar posts have gained traction for you before? Are you posting that photo because you like it, or because you know it will do well at 8 p.m. on a Sunday with a specific caption style? These are not paranoid questions. They are daily negotiations that users navigate—often unconsciously—as they balance the desire for authentic expression with the realities of platform logic. *Visibility is not merely an outcome; it is a design lever that reshapes behaviour.*

This has psychological consequences. When identity is crafted through performance under algorithmic surveillance, it introduces a persistent tension between self and strategy. Users may experience what researchers call *context collapse*: the compression of multiple audiences (friends, strangers, employers, algorithmic filters) into a single point of expression. The result is self-censorship, strategic ambiguity, or the creation of parallel identities—Finstas, alt accounts, burner profiles—where the stakes feel lower. Yet even these spaces are not immune. As soon as a platform detects engagement patterns, it begins to optimise. What was once authentic can rapidly become performative simply through feedback.

The pursuit of visibility also carries asymmetrical costs. Users who already fit dominant platform norms—visually appealing, socioeconomically privileged, charismatic, ideologically conformist—are more likely to succeed with minimal distortion. Those outside those norms must work harder to be seen, often contorting their self-presentation in ways that replicate social inequalities. A Black woman on YouTube may feel pressured to adopt a performative affect to gain traction in a space where whiteness and "relatability" are implicitly rewarded. A queer teenager on Instagram may hide aspects of their identity to avoid algorithmic deboosting or harassment. In this way, *performance is not merely aesthetic—it is sociopolitical.* The cost of visibility is not distributed evenly.

There is also the question of memory. On platforms where performance is perpetual, the past becomes a liability. Posts that no longer reflect one's beliefs, tone, or identity may resurface algorithmically at any time, recontextualised without consent. The pressure to manage this digital trail—to prune, archive, delete, or rebrand—adds another layer to the performance. The self is not only curated for now, but continuously audited for future risk. *Authenticity becomes a liability when the system has no memory for change.*

And yet, platforms frame this entire dynamic as empowerment. "Build your personal brand," "Monetise your passion," "Be your own boss"—these slogans suggest autonomy, when in fact they often describe a form of *platform-dependent labour*. Visibility, influence, and audience are mediated not by community consensus, but by algorithmic systems that are opaque, unaccountable, and volatile. A user may spend months refining their content strategy only to have a platform tweak its feed logic, rendering that work obsolete. The self, once offered for connection, becomes a product subject to the whims of machine-led distribution.

Still, many users find meaning in this ecosystem. Performance, after all, is not inherently inauthentic. It can be creative, playful, strategic. The problem arises when systems *conflate performance with identity,* personalisation with insight, and engagement with value. The more these conflations solidify, the harder it becomes to recognise where the algorithm ends and the self begins. *To perform for the feed is to trade a measure of authenticity for a currency denominated in visibility—a currency whose value is determined by machines, not meaning.*

The long-term risk is not just exhaustion or distortion, but *disempowerment.* When platforms shape what is seen, and when what is seen shapes how we act, users may gradually lose touch with the distinction between what is chosen and what is prompted. The desire to be seen becomes a vector of influence. Identity becomes a speculative asset: invested in, adjusted, rebranded, and sometimes liquidated, all in service of platform logic.

There is no simple remedy. But clarity is a start. Understanding the mechanics behind the feed—the performative incentives, the data-driven conditioning, the selective amplification—makes space for reflection. It allows for a more deliberate engagement with platforms: to perform, perhaps, but with awareness; to curate, but with agency; to be seen, but not defined by what is shown.

The challenge, then, is not to reject performance outright, but to ask: *whose gaze are we performing for, and at what cost?* When visibility becomes the primary validator of value, when the feed governs the contours of expression, when the algorithm becomes our most attentive audience—it is time to pause. Because the most radical act in a system optimised for performance may simply be *to speak in a voice it cannot predict*.

Social Mirrors and Behavioural Loops

The self is no longer just lived; it is now performed, recorded, reacted to, and recalibrated—often in real time. Social media has become the mirror in which individuals glimpse not only how they appear but also how they are valued. The interface between digital feedback and personal behaviour is no longer a point of contact—it is a loop, a recursive circuit in which action invites reaction, and reaction reshapes future action. *To participate in digital culture is to internalise metrics, recalibrate expression, and—over time—reshape one's very identity in response to the data one receives.*

The architecture of platforms like Instagram, TikTok, Twitter, Facebook, and Snapchat is not passive. These systems do more than transmit messages; they actively format experience. A post is no longer a gesture but a test. A tweet is not simply speech—it is a probe into the social field, a way to gauge resonance, relevance, or rejection. The interface responds with likes, retweets, shares, comments, and view counts, metrics which—while ostensibly neutral—carry deep emotional weight. A teenager deletes a photo that didn't perform. A comedian edits their voice to chase virality. A political commentator doubles down on outrage because it elicits a reliable uptick in engagement. *The logic of social mirrors is cumulative, not incidental. It builds behavioural architecture over time.*

What distinguishes digital feedback from traditional forms of social reinforcement is its scale, speed, and permanence. In a pre-digital context, feedback from others was typically slow, partial, and bounded by context. Today, reactions are instantaneous, quantified, and public. A comment section is not a conversation; it is a spectacle of judgement. This scale amplifies psychological effects. A minor critique, when delivered by hundreds of strangers, can feel like a referendum on one's identity. A rush of approval, even for a trivial post, may be interpreted as proof of validation. The danger is not in any single interaction, but in *how repeated exposure to these signals conditions future behaviour*.

The phenomenon is perhaps most visible in young users, for whom adolescence—a period already marked by identity exploration—is now entangled with platforms optimised for feedback. Research from institutions such as the Royal Society for Public Health in the UK and Pew Research Center in the US confirms a rising correlation between social media use and increased anxiety, self-monitoring, and self-objectification. But to treat this as a matter of "teenage insecurity" is to misunderstand the structural dimension. The entire system is engineered to elicit, surface, and rank social signals. That these signals affect self-conception is not a bug—it is the platform's behavioural economy in action.

The loop works as follows: a user posts content—an image, a thought, a short video. That content is exposed to a network of viewers. Based on performance (measured in engagement metrics), the user infers which versions of themselves are rewarded. Future posts are adjusted accordingly. This adjustment is rarely explicit. It may appear as a slight shift in tone, a new angle in a selfie, a more provocative caption. But over time, these micro-adjustments add up to a broader transformation. *The person becomes a projection of what the system has taught them is acceptable, attractive, or shareable.*

This behavioural shaping is not just personal—it is cultural. Consider how meme formats evolve on Twitter: a structure goes viral, is repeated, remixed, and saturated, until the platform's attention shifts. Users participate in this cycle not only to express themselves, but to remain visible. Or think about TikTok's dance trends: users replicate movements, expressions, and rhythms not just for creative expression, but to ride the wave of algorithmic distribution. *Originality is tolerated only insofar as it conforms to recognisable forms.* This is not to say creativity is absent—indeed, constraints can foster innovation. But it is a creativity disciplined by the demand for resonance.

One of the more subtle effects of these behavioural loops is the erosion of interiority. When expression becomes externalised and optimised for reaction, it becomes harder to distinguish between what one genuinely believes and what one has learned to perform. A person may share a political opinion not because they hold it deeply, but because similar posts have attracted support. They may amplify a grievance because previous outrage increased their following. Over time, *the mirror begins to shape the face*. Self-perception becomes co-authored by digital feedback, which serves as a proxy for value, truth, and identity.

The issue is compounded by the asymmetry of the loop. The user offers vulnerability—emotion, belief, effort. The platform responds not with care or nuance, but with metrics. There is no meaningful dialogue, no contextual understanding, no space for missteps or ambiguity. The algorithm rewards engagement, not empathy. This distorts how people behave, especially in moments of conflict or vulnerability. A heartfelt post that sparks debate may be ranked higher than a reflective one that fosters quiet thought. The system equates response with value, but *not all feedback is wisdom, and not all reaction is worth internalising*.

Moreover, behavioural loops do not just affect what we *share*—they affect what we *consume*. Recommendation engines tailor content based on previous engagement, meaning users are shown more of what they have liked, clicked, or paused on before. This subtly nudges attention toward familiar patterns, reinforcing existing preferences and biases. The feedback loop thus extends beyond expression to perception. One's worldview becomes algorithmically affirmed, leading to what scholars have termed "confirmation bubbles" or "algorithmic enclaves." Users receive more of what affirms them and less of what challenges them—not by conscious choice, but by systemic design. *The social mirror reflects not only who we are, but what we expect to see.*

Of course, not every user succumbs equally to these dynamics. Some cultivate detachment, irony, or critical distance. Others deliberately manipulate the system, using fake engagement to boost content or masking their true opinions behind alt accounts. But even these forms of resistance acknowledge the system's power. The fact that one must strategise around the loop, rather than ignore it, attests to its influence. The behavioural loop is not only a psychological force; it is an infrastructural fact.

What makes this loop so powerful is its subtlety. It doesn't demand conformity—it rewards it. It doesn't ban dissent—it demotes it. It doesn't impose identity—it incentivises a version of the self most palatable to the system. Over time, the distinction between the self and its mirror image begins to dissolve. And yet, *because the mirror reflects us, we mistake its logic for our own*. We internalise not only the attention we receive, but the values embedded in the mechanisms that structure that attention.

There are real social consequences to this. Activism morphs into performative allyship, shaped more by optics than action. Public discourse becomes polarised, not because people are inherently extreme, but because platforms amplify sharpness over subtlety. Emotional labour is extracted for clout, then discarded. Even friendship is gamified: who replies fastest, who posts most, who reacts visibly. These are not moral failings of users—they are predictable outcomes of systems that *monetise visibility and reward behavioural conformity.*

The question, then, is not simply how to resist, but how to recognise. How do we become aware of the mirrors we're performing into, and how do we break the loop without disappearing from view? The answer lies less in withdrawal than in literacy: understanding how platforms shape perception, noticing when expression becomes reflex, and reclaiming the space to act outside prediction. Because the most dangerous mirrors are not the ones that distort, but the ones that convince us they are neutral.

In a world of behavioural loops, maintaining agency begins with stepping outside the circuit—if only long enough to ask whether we are still speaking for ourselves, or merely echoing back what the mirror expects to hear.

Agency in the Age of the Feed

There is a paradox at the heart of contemporary digital life: the more we try to be seen, the less we remain ourselves. Social media feeds—the algorithmic scaffolds of attention—offer users unprecedented visibility, yet the terms of that visibility are rarely their own. What appears to be self-expression is often a strategic performance, calibrated not for authenticity but for alignment with opaque algorithms that decide who gets heard, liked, or shared. In this environment, *being seen means being shaped*. The algorithm doesn't just curate our content; it contours our behaviour. The urgent question is no longer just how to be visible—but whether it's still possible to be self-directed when platforms are designed to reward predictability over personality.

At its core, agency means the ability to act with intention. It is not merely freedom from external control, but the power to choose how one engages, responds, and evolves. Yet on feed-driven platforms, the agency of users is often transmuted into a series of reactive loops. Every like, share, and view contributes to a behavioural ledger that predicts what one might do next. In turn, the system reinforces patterns it deems successful, nudging users toward content and conduct that maximises engagement—by its definition. Over time, the feed becomes a feedback chamber, not just reflecting what we like, but subtly reshaping what we are likely to like. *The illusion of choice masks a subtle form of behavioural nudging*. This is not coercion in the traditional sense, but a soft orchestration of attention and expression that is no less powerful for its subtlety.

The architecture of platforms encourages users to collapse the gap between persona and performance. To be visible is to be favoured by the algorithm; to be favoured by the algorithm is to follow its unspoken rules. This fosters a digital survivalism where users tailor their output to match what the system rewards—shorter videos, bolder thumbnails, faster punchlines. What begins as creative engagement mutates into a narrow optimisation problem.

Creators learn to suppress nuance and flatten complexity in service of immediacy. The feed doesn't have patience for context; it hungers for click-throughs, hooks, and heat. And the effect is not limited to influencers or content producers. Even everyday users feel the tug. Posts are written with potential reactions in mind, moments are captured not for memory but for metrics, and silence feels like erasure in an ecosystem that equates visibility with validity.

Crucially, this environment conditions users to internalise external metrics as internal measures of worth. The platform doesn't merely reflect social value—it prescribes it. A tweet that garners traction feels more "right" than one that languishes unseen. A post that earns engagement subtly retrofits itself into the user's memory as a good idea, regardless of original intent. Over time, *we begin to trust platform feedback more than our private instincts*. This is not because we are gullible, but because digital validation is fast, frequent, and culturally reinforced. The feed becomes a mirror, and we start adjusting our self-image to fit what we see reflected there.

Yet what makes the issue especially insidious is the design of the feed itself. Unlike traditional media, feeds are dynamic, personalised, and inescapably ambient. There is no neutral baseline, no shared sequence. Two users may open the same app and encounter completely different realities—crafted not by editorial judgement but by statistical inference. This creates what sociologist Zeynep Tufekci has called "algorithmic gatekeeping," a process where machine learning determines visibility based on previous engagement patterns. But unlike traditional gatekeepers—editors, curators, educators—algorithms do not explain their choices. They do not justify omissions or admit bias. Their authority is *procedural,* not deliberative, and their influence pervasive yet invisible. *We navigate curated spaces without knowing who is doing the curating or why.*

To reclaim agency in this context requires a reorientation of how we interact with platforms—not just technically, but psychologically. Some users have adopted counterstrategies: posting less frequently, consuming passively, or creating alternate profiles. Others attempt algorithmic disruption—liking atypical content, diversifying follows, resisting the impulse to engage with outrage. These are small gestures, but they matter. Each act of digital resistance interrupts the cycle of reactive behaviour and reasserts the user as a self-aware participant rather than a passive endpoint. But such strategies demand a level of literacy that few are taught. *Algorithmic literacy*—the ability to understand, question, and strategically navigate recommendation systems—should no longer be considered optional. It is a civic skill for the age of the feed.

That said, the burden of agency cannot rest solely on users. Platforms are not neutral spaces—they are engineered environments, designed to elicit certain behaviours and discourage others. While they may claim to empower, they often exploit. The asymmetry of knowledge is stark: users provide data; platforms process and profit from it. Users receive notifications; platforms receive insights. Even transparency efforts—"why am I seeing this post?"—often obfuscate more than they illuminate, offering superficial explanations that conceal the true depth of algorithmic inference. The real calculus is buried in proprietary code, inaccessible to scrutiny and immune to negotiation. Until platform governance includes meaningful accountability and user oversight, any discussion of digital agency remains partial.

Philosophically, this returns us to a long-standing tension: the conflict between autonomy and design. Can one truly act freely within a system that shapes one's perceptions, preferences, and possibilities? The ancient Stoics suggested that freedom lies not in external conditions but in internal clarity. Yet in digital environments, internal clarity is difficult to cultivate when one's intuitions are shaped by algorithmic reinforcement. In this light, reclaiming agency means cultivating an intentional posture toward digital life—*a posture of deliberate awareness rather than automatic participation*. It is not about abandoning platforms, but about refusing to be silently enrolled in systems that do not disclose their aims.

Ultimately, the goal is not purity, but balance. Visibility has its uses, and curation is not inherently inauthentic. But when visibility becomes the sole currency, and curation replaces reflection, the cost is not just privacy or time—it is identity itself. The feed may be the medium, but the self remains the message. Whether we allow it to be distorted or directed is the real terrain of choice. To live with agency in the age of the feed is to *remember that attention is not just a resource—it is an act of will.*

Chapter 8
Friction as Freedom

Speed has become the altar to which contemporary digital design bows. Every scroll, swipe, click, and tap is meticulously engineered for seamlessness—resistance minimised, hesitation erased, every interaction smoothed until choice itself is reduced to impulse. Convenience masquerades as progress, and good design is measured in the absence of friction. Yet beneath this doctrine of efficiency lies a subtle, insidious cost: the erosion of reflective pause, the diminishing of agency sharpened by deliberation. Perhaps the very interruptions we seek to eliminate are what make our choices meaningful. Perhaps slowing down is not a barrier to freedom, but its prerequisite.

Friction—those small pauses, confirmation prompts, or mental demands—is often treated as a design flaw to be excised. One-click purchases, autoplay videos, endless feeds: the race is to remove steps between desire and gratification. The less you feel the mechanics, the more "frictionless" the experience, the better, supposedly. Yet this obsession overlooks a crucial truth: friction is often where freedom resides. The hesitation before a purchase, the second glance at a headline, the act of typing rather than tapping—these are not inefficiencies. They are opportunities. Invitations to pause, reconsider, or say no.

Modern interfaces, by contrast, are designed to bypass contemplation. Consider subscription cancellations, where entering is trivial but exiting resembles a labyrinth. Or the endlessly scrolling social feed, which proceeds without pause or consent. These are deliberate choices, calibrated to reduce exit points and sustain engagement. The objective is not merely presence, but reaction—not deciding, but drifting. Online interaction subtly redefines action: to engage is increasingly to submit, not select. Authentic agency in this context demands resistance; resistance demands friction.

Slowness, then, is not a flaw of digital decision-making—it is its foundation. Philosophers have long linked deliberation to liberty. Aristotle argued that freedom is not the absence of constraint but the capacity for reasoned choice. To act rightly, one must reflect. This resonates acutely in a digital age where attention is monetised and decisions are measured as conversions. A fast choice is not necessarily a free one. True autonomy emerges not from speed but from depth of thought. Slowness is not laziness; it is sovereignty.

Yet advocating for friction is not romanticising inefficiency. It is reclaiming cognitive effort as a medium of significance. Some tasks warrant difficulty. Some moments demand discomfort. Not because struggle is virtuous in itself, but because effort signals value. A carefully composed email requires more than a thumbs-up emoji, but it yields clarity, intention, and relational depth. Making an informed choice—about news, finances, or relationships—requires cognitive investment. Difficulty here is not a flaw but a feature. When all is easy, nothing is earned.

Designers of humane technology are beginning to recognise this subtle truth. Browsers such as Brave, or extensions like Momentum, deliberately interrupt habitual behaviour—delaying access to addictive sites or transforming blank tabs into reminders of intention. Platforms like Centered or

Freedom reintroduce control over attention and time. These are not digital retreats; they are invitations to pause within the stream, not escape from it. The aim is conscious re-entry, a practice of selective friction.

This chapter explores friction not as inconvenience but as a moral and cognitive affordance. Interruptions can serve as protective buffers; complexity can cultivate discernment; effort can anchor attention in meaning. We examine systems that restore deliberation: timers requiring confirmation before sending an email, read-later defaults, or platforms that intentionally limit content exposure. These interventions are contemporary forms of self-defence, restoring intentionality within ecosystems optimised for speed and scale.

The goal is not wholesale rejection of technology but conscious re-engagement. Complete withdrawal from digital life is neither realistic nor desirable. The task is cultivating habits of selective engagement: recognising when friction is necessary, when streamlining is preferable, when cognitive cost is valuable, and when automation is beneficial. The operative word is choice. Friction, when chosen, empowers rather than obstructs.

In many respects, this marks the next frontier of digital maturity—not faster productivity, but wiser, slower choice. The question is not how to escape the system, but how to recalibrate our relationship to it. Where has speed eclipsed substance? Where has automation displaced agency? And where might friction quietly restore both? This chapter is a guide to reclaiming that space—not as resistance to progress, but as the fertile ground in which authentic freedom can take root.

The Case for Slowness

Modern interface design tends to equate speed with success. Everything from a one-click purchase to infinite scrolling aims to reduce friction—minimising the number of steps, thoughts, or seconds between impulse and action. But the unspoken cost of this seamlessness is agency. The slower path, once associated with careful thought and discernment, is now framed as inefficiency or inconvenience. Yet beneath this friction lies something essential: the capacity for choice that is truly ours.

To move slowly, deliberately, even awkwardly through an interface or decision is not a design flaw; it's a space for freedom. When a system interrupts us—asks us to confirm, reflect, pause—it may be rescuing us from the automation of impulse. This is especially vital in a world where platforms are engineered to anticipate and satisfy our wants before we're even aware of them. A smooth experience often disguises the fact that the choices it accelerates have already been structured, nudged, or pre-selected. *Speed does not merely reduce effort; it can pre-empt agency.*

The deliberate use of friction in design is not new. In aviation and medicine, friction is built in as a safeguard. Pilots must double-confirm commands to avoid catastrophic errors. Surgeons pause for procedural time-outs to verify identity, site, and plan before beginning an operation. These systems understand that human beings make better decisions when they have the opportunity to reconsider. In digital environments, however, friction is often seen as a barrier to engagement. This ethos has become dominant across consumer platforms, where the ultimate goal is retention, not reflection.

Consider the design of a checkout process in an online store. Reducing clicks is treated as a victory. But what is lost when the decision to buy becomes indistinguishable from a tap? Compare this with the now largely abandoned "shopping cart" metaphor of early e-commerce: once, a user could collect items, review them later, and reconsider before confirming. Now, swiping right on a product, video, or person can trigger a chain of consequences with no frictional pause. *We are encouraged to act faster than we can reflect.*

Psychologists have long noted that effort is not always a deterrent—sometimes, it enhances perceived value. This is the principle behind the "IKEA effect": people assign more worth to things they've invested effort in assembling. Similarly, when a belief or decision is hard-won—when it requires wrestling with conflicting data, ambiguity, or delayed gratification—it becomes more integrated into a person's identity. In contrast, beliefs formed through instantaneous affirmation, especially within echo chambers or curated feeds, may lack the stability or depth of genuinely held convictions. *Friction is not only a gatekeeper of agency but a cultivator of meaning.*

The current paradigm of "frictionless design" treats users as optimisers—constantly seeking to maximise convenience and minimise exertion. But this view flattens the full range of human experience. People are not simply consumers of efficiency; they are also makers of meaning. We do not only want what is fastest; we often want what is right, considered, or beautiful. The design principle that aligns most closely with this reality is not optimisation, but invitation: the creation of environments where choice is honoured, not hurried.

This argument becomes even more urgent when we look at recommendation algorithms and default settings. The default is rarely neutral. In platforms like YouTube or TikTok, what follows "next" is not chosen by the user but by an opaque system of engagement prediction. Even search engines, once thought of as passive indexes, are now ranked, ranked again, and prioritised to drive behavioural outcomes. In such spaces, slowness becomes resistance. The act of scrolling back, searching differently, or asking "why this result?" is itself a reclamation of control.

Of course, friction must be designed with intention, not imposed indiscriminately. Poorly implemented friction frustrates without enlightening. But reflective friction—delays that are meaningful, prompts that provoke reconsideration, pathways that allow for exit and re-entry—can reintroduce a sense of authorship over our decisions. In the same way that a good teacher does not rush to the answer but lets the student struggle productively, good systems respect the intelligence and autonomy of the user by not overly smoothing the way.

One illuminating example comes from mindfulness and mental health apps, some of which deliberately slow the user's interaction. Before beginning a meditation, users are prompted with a few deep breaths or asked to reflect on their intent. These pauses are more than just aesthetic. They scaffold a different relationship to the activity—anchoring it in reflection rather than consumption. Even the Apple Watch's "Breathe" reminder—a small act of deceleration—works not because it tells you to breathe, but because it interrupts the rhythm of non-stop attention that defines the digital day. *Interruptions, if designed well, are invitations back to presence.*

Choice overload, a closely related issue, is often seen as the enemy of action. Yet not all overload is paralysing. The problem arises not from the number of options, but from the context in which they're presented. Netflix, for example, offers seemingly endless possibilities but little structural support for meaningful choice. In contrast, a well-designed museum, though equally full of content, guides visitors through curated sequences that leave space for detours and contemplation. The difference lies in whether the system is optimised for passive consumption or for active exploration.

Slowness also matters politically. When civic participation—voting, signing petitions, reading legislation—is reduced to a click, the citizen becomes a user, and the public sphere turns transactional. Consider the digitalisation of town halls into Twitter threads, or of protest into hashtag trends. These transformations are not inherently bad, but they risk trading deliberation for visibility. *A society that acts faster than it can think soon begins to confuse amplification with consensus.*

Importantly, the antidote is not nostalgia for a pre-digital age. The goal is not to rewind history, but to upgrade our mental models. Slowness today is not simply about avoiding digital speed; it's about *redefining the value of effort in an age of automation.* Just as slow food is not about cooking inefficiency but about cultivating relationship to food and land, slow interfaces are about restoring relationship to self and choice.

Designers, developers, and product managers hold substantial power in this space. But so do users. Every choice not to click the first link, not to autoplay the next video, not to swipe reflexively, is an act of cognitive friction. These small resistances accumulate. They form habits of attention. They teach the mind that it is not merely reacting to a feed, but shaping its contours.

The question is not how to eliminate friction but how to use it wisely. When friction is designed to prompt inquiry, to allow escape from defaults, to introduce doubt or nuance, it becomes a tool of emancipation. *Slowness is not the enemy of progress—it is often its precondition.* In a culture obsessed with the fast, the frictionless, and the friction-free, it may be the slowest gesture—pausing before acting—that holds the greatest power.

Designing for Deliberation

In an age where immediacy is often mistaken for efficiency, design has become the invisible architect of behaviour. Interfaces increasingly function not merely as neutral channels but as cues—gentle, persistent prompts that shape not just what we do, but how we think. While the dominant ethos of Silicon Valley prizes frictionless engagement, rapid throughput, and maximised "flow," a quiet resistance is emerging. It contends that slowness, reflection, and discomfort are not bugs in the system but essential features for a flourishing, autonomous mind. This is the case for designing digital experiences that prioritise deliberation over momentum, and nuance over nudge.

Consider the ubiquitous "swipe right" mechanism of dating apps. It offers what feels like agency—decide quickly, act instantly—but the entire structure is calibrated to suppress deeper consideration. There's no invitation to pause, no friction to compel users to ask, "What am I really looking for?" or "Why did I reject that face?" The interface becomes a conveyor belt of micro-decisions whose significance is disguised by their speed. *When design encourages velocity, it discourages reflection.*

The alternative lies not in romanticising inefficiency, but in redefining what efficiency is for. The purpose of an interface should not be to eliminate thought, but to steward it. This is where deliberative design enters the conversation. These are systems crafted not to hijack attention but to slow it down purposefully—to make space for cognitive friction, moral hesitance, and epistemic humility. Rather than driving engagement through dopamine loops and predictive personalisation, deliberative tools interrupt the loop. They create pause points: carefully engineered intervals that reintroduce thought into decision-making.

Take the example of the open-source browser extension "Tranquility." When installed, it doesn't block websites. It doesn't shame the user or alarm them with their screen-time statistics. Instead, it overlays the interface with a single reflective prompt: *What brought you here today?* The effect is subtle but profound. It doesn't impose friction in the form of delays or popups but introduces a layer of internalised awareness. It creates a dissonance—a moment of cognitive contrast between the habitual impulse and a deliberate goal. *That brief window is often all it takes to turn consumption into consideration.*

Designing for deliberation is fundamentally about the calibration of attention. Attention is not a commodity, as the advertising economy suggests, but a capacity—an ability to dwell, to discern, to choose with care. Interfaces that are shaped with this philosophy at their core tend to do several things differently. They foreground content over engagement metrics. They make hidden system choices transparent—surfacing the logic behind algorithmic recommendations or ranking criteria. They resist infinite scrolls and dark patterns in favour of bounded experiences and clear exits. Their structure assumes the user is capable of mature thought, not merely vulnerable to behavioural triggers.

This design philosophy finds an ally in some emerging educational technologies. Consider the platform "Perusall," which allows students to collaboratively annotate texts, not in the margins of their own minds, but in the company of peers. Instead of gamifying participation through point systems, it uses structured dialogue to reward thoughtful engagement. Students are not prompted to "complete the reading" but to deepen the reading. The interface slows them down through interaction, not obstacle—nudging them to process, synthesise, and challenge. It's a lesson in how structure can serve intellect rather than override it.

Yet, the challenge of deliberative design is not only technical; it is cultural. The dominant UX paradigm rewards what's called "conversion"—turning a glance into a click, a user into a buyer. Within such systems, every pause is a potential lost sale, every hesitation a metric to be minimised. This is why so few mainstream platforms incorporate design-for-deliberation principles: *their business models cannot afford your attention to linger in thought.* The attention economy thrives on impulsivity because it monetises prediction. Reflective users are unpredictable users—harder to funnel, slower to profile.

What's required, then, is a more expansive definition of value. Just as we no longer see calories alone as a measure of nutritional goodness, so too must we move beyond clicks and engagement time as indicators of platform success. A well-designed interface should not only facilitate decisions—it should elevate them. Deliberative design reframes interaction not as friction to overcome, but as an opportunity to engage the whole person—cognitive, emotional, ethical. It repositions the user not as a passive consumer of choices, but as an active co-author of outcomes.

Designing for deliberation also asks difficult questions about accessibility and privilege. Who has the time to pause? Who has the literacy to decode interface cues or question algorithmic logic? If slow design becomes a luxury for the few—offered only in boutique apps for knowledge workers or niche productivity tools—then its promise is partial at best. For deliberation to scale, it must be built into defaults, not bolted on as an option for those already inclined to use it. Public institutions, educational platforms, civic tools, and even e-commerce systems have a role to play in creating environments where deliberation is the norm, not the exception.

The stakes of this conversation extend beyond UX. At a societal level, we are witnessing the erosion of deliberative capacity itself—in political discourse, institutional trust, and the architecture of public reason. The infrastructure of fast, polarised, emotionally charged interaction is not just exhausting; it is epistemically corrosive. It dulls the mind's appetite for complexity. Designing for deliberation is, in this context, a form of civic repair. It rebuilds the cognitive habits that democracy depends on: slow thinking, reasoned disagreement, provisional belief.

Even the most habitual technologies can be retrofitted to support this aim. Email clients like "Hey" have begun integrating reflective triage systems that prompt users to decide not just what to read, but when and why. Social media platforms with chronological timelines and manual curation options (such as Mastodon or certain subreddits) offer glimpses of environments where the user reclaims navigational authority. These examples remain on the margins, but they are not isolated. They point to a design ecology in which reflection competes with reflex, and sometimes wins.

Designing for deliberation is not a nostalgic appeal to slower times, nor a rejection of digital convenience. It is a clear-eyed recognition that *agency is shaped by design*, and that the freedom to choose well requires space in which to think clearly. As platforms become more immersive, as choices become more algorithmically scaffolded, and as interfaces become more anticipatory, the need for deliberative design will only grow more urgent.

We do not need to abandon frictionless experiences altogether. But we must learn to discern when speed is serving us and when it is undermining us. Not all interruptions are annoyances; some are invitations. Not all effort is inefficiency; sometimes it is wisdom. And not all attention should be captured; some of it deserves to be cultivated. Designing for deliberation is, at heart, a commitment to treating users not as data points but as thinking beings—capable not just of choice, but of judgment.

Reclaiming Cognitive Costs

The prevailing logic of digital design tells us that effort is undesirable. Friction, delay, and mental exertion are framed as failures of the system—errors to be engineered out. But what if this narrative is not only incomplete, but actively corrosive to our autonomy and discernment? What if some cognitive costs are worth paying—not because they are pleasurable or efficient, but because they are formative? To reclaim cognitive cost is not to glorify complexity for its own sake, but to recognise that ease is not neutral. Simplicity, when manufactured by technology, often conceals the invisible shaping of thought, taste, and choice. In bypassing difficulty, we may also bypass depth.

One of the foundational insights from behavioural economics is that humans are cognitive misers. We prefer heuristics to heavy reasoning, defaults to decisions, swipes to scrutiny. This is not a flaw—it's a feature of how we conserve mental energy in complex environments. But the digital age has not merely accommodated this tendency; it has industrialised it. Algorithms, recommendation engines, auto-complete prompts, and personalisation systems all function to minimise cognitive labour. The outcome is a user experience optimised for frictionlessness—and a populace increasingly habituated to externalised thinking.

This has consequences that are not just individual but civic. When every menu is personalised, when every option is pre-ranked, when every interaction is made seamless, we are not simply saving time. We are forfeiting encounters with ambiguity, resistance, and deliberation—the very moments where critical faculties are forged. *Effort, in this sense, is not a tax on cognition but a training ground for it.* And yet, this principle remains largely absent from the design philosophies that shape our most used tools.

Consider the rise of "one-click" culture. From purchasing a book to ordering a meal to expressing political sentiment, digital systems have condensed complex behaviours into minimal actions. This has undeniable utility. But it also collapses distinction. When the cognitive cost of buying a novel and signing a petition are functionally equivalent, the underlying processes—economic, moral, social—become flattened. *We perform the action without absorbing its implications.* By removing friction, platforms remove reflection. And reflection, though costly, is the crucible of meaningful engagement.

This is not an argument for regress or nostalgia. It is not a call to make interfaces obtuse or labyrinthine. Rather, it is an invitation to reimagine cognitive cost as a resource to be shaped, not a liability to be erased. Just as physical resistance strengthens muscle, cognitive effort cultivates discernment. The philosopher Daniel Kahneman draws a line between "System 1" thinking—fast, automatic, intuitive—and "System 2" thinking—slow, effortful, analytical. What our digital environments overwhelmingly do is optimise for System 1. The result is not stupidity but superficiality: users who are competent, but disengaged.

There are, however, systems that deliberately preserve cognitive cost. Wikipedia's editorial infrastructure is a prime example. Unlike platforms that prioritise speed or simplicity, Wikipedia requires contributors to navigate layers of policy, cite sources, and engage in open deliberation. It is not an easy platform to shape. And that difficulty, that architecture of care, is what gives it epistemic credibility. *The cost of contributing becomes the price of trust.*

Educational technologies offer another arena where effort is being reframed. Consider the design of active recall systems like Anki or spaced repetition tools used in medical and legal training. These platforms explicitly *make learning harder*—not to frustrate users but to deepen retention. The difficulty is not an oversight. It is the method. In this context, cognitive cost is not the enemy of learning; it is its medium.

Yet such examples remain the exception. Most mainstream systems continue to equate user satisfaction with ease. This is why "cognitive overload" is treated as a pathology and "low-friction UX" as a virtue. But overload and effort are not synonymous. *Overload is a result of poor structuring; effort is the result of meaningful engagement.* The former is overwhelming; the latter is developmental. Good cognitive cost—what we might call constructive friction—does not swamp the user. It stretches them.

The implications extend beyond interface design into how we understand knowledge itself. When Google autocompletes our queries, when Spotify curates our playlists, when social platforms recommend what to read, we outsource not just information-gathering but curiosity itself. *The mind becomes a consumer of conclusions rather than a seeker of context.* By reinstating cognitive effort—through prompts, constraints, or layered exploration—we can recover the epistemic virtues of attention, patience, and doubt.

Indeed, not all difficulty is virtuous. Poor design, unnecessary complexity, or bureaucratic inertia can impose unproductive costs. But it is precisely by distinguishing between *productive* and *destructive* friction that we begin to develop a more mature design ethics. The goal is not to make systems harder, but to make users deeper. This requires design that trusts the user—not to always know what they want, but to be capable of growing into that knowledge through challenge.

A good example of this is the writing software "Scrivener." It offers complexity not for show, but for structure. Unlike minimalist editors that strip away options in pursuit of elegance, Scrivener allows for layering, scaffolding, and modular thinking. It assumes that the user's task—longform composition—is cognitively demanding, and it meets that demand with tools that respect it. *Here, complexity becomes a form of dignity.*

Even in commercial contexts, the reintroduction of cognitive cost can enhance—not diminish—value. Take the example of luxury e-commerce sites that require multiple verification steps, longer onboarding processes, or appointment-only browsing. These friction points are not bugs but features: they signal deliberation, exclusivity, and care. They are signals that the transaction is not mere consumption but commitment. The effort signals investment.

So what would it mean to build more digital spaces around this principle? It would mean designing platforms that sometimes *ask more* of their users, not less. It would mean replacing "Are you sure?" with "Why are you sure?" It would mean creating decision architectures that expose trade-offs rather than hiding them. It would mean showing provenance, not just output. And it would mean valuing the user not only as a point of engagement, but as a mind in development.

Reclaiming cognitive cost is thus an act of intellectual respect. It tells the user: you are capable of hard thought. You are worthy of complexity. You are more than your clicks. In a digital world bent on making everything frictionless, this message is quietly radical. And, perhaps, urgently necessary.

How to Opt Back In, Selectively

The call to "unplug" has become almost performative—a digital detox, a weekend retreat, a phone buried in a drawer as symbolic protest. But abstention is not strategy. While temporary disconnection may provide relief, it rarely delivers sustained clarity or restored agency. What's needed is not blanket avoidance but intentional re-entry. Not an escape from technology, but *a refined relationship to it*. The future belongs not to those who log off entirely, but to those who learn how to *opt back in—selectively, consciously, and on their own terms*.

Selective re-engagement begins by recognising that technologies are not neutral channels, but environments with logics of their own. To participate in them without reflex is to become fluent in a language you never chose. Yet rejecting them wholesale forfeits the civic, professional, and social power they confer. A more sustainable posture is one of cultivated friction—where the goal is not minimal screen time, but maximal alignment between *use* and *intention*.

Consider, for instance, the difference between *habitual* and *deliberate* use. Opening Instagram to fill a silence is qualitatively distinct from opening it to view a saved post on climate data visualisation. The same tool, two different trajectories of attention. The selective user engineers their digital environment to support the latter—*not by resisting distraction endlessly, but by designing it out upfront*. Tools like browser extensions that hide feeds, email clients that batch notifications, or apps that delay access to attention sinks do not reduce connectivity. They reshape it. They reintroduce *choice architecture* into a landscape built for compulsion.

There is a growing ecosystem of tools and practices that support such re-engagement. The mindfulness platform *Balance* doesn't merely guide meditation—it tailors audio sessions to individual stress patterns and attention spans. The note-taking app *Obsidian* eschews cloud-centric, feed-style capture in favour of a local, networked interface designed for deep, long-form thinking. These aren't simply *alternatives* to the mainstream platforms; they embody a different ethic: one that treats the user not as a data point, but as a mind in development.

Importantly, opting back in does not mean returning to previous digital habits with new vocabulary. It means re-encountering the ecosystem with a revised set of values and questions. *Is this platform helping me think better? Is it expanding my view or narrowing it? Is it enabling participation or reinforcing dependence?* These are not rhetorical queries—they are diagnostics. They clarify whether engagement is aligned or extractive. And they are the foundation of a selective digital ethic.

Take the example of news consumption. The standard model—a mix of outrage, novelty, and social performance—rewards reaction over comprehension. But it is possible to re-engage differently. Subscribing to slower, context-driven outlets like *Tortoise*, or setting structured time each week to review diverse sources, changes both the emotional and epistemic texture of news. *You are no longer grazing; you are cultivating*. This shift reclaims one's attention from the timeline without abandoning the public sphere.

Another domain ripe for selective re-engagement is personal communication. Messaging apps often collapse boundaries between intimacy, logistics, and obligation. A weekend text from a colleague arrives alongside a meme from a sibling, and both share screen real estate with urgent group chats. The result is a continuity of stimulus but a fragmentation of presence. One way forward is *channel separation*—using different apps for different relational modes (e.g. Signal for close friends, email for asynchronous coordination, Slack for professional flow). By doing so, the user restores *contextual integrity* to their interactions. It is not disconnection—it is reclassification.

The underlying principle here is that *not all engagements are created equal*. Being online is not a monolith. There is a difference between *broadcasting* and *building,* between *scrolling* and *studying,* between *availability* and *accessibility.* Selective re-engagement means evaluating each platform, tool, or stream according to what it enables—and what it costs.

Crucially, this evaluation is not purely personal. It is infrastructural. To selectively re-engage also means recognising how interfaces shape our agency. Default settings, feed ordering, nudging patterns, and engagement metrics—all these design choices subtly steer behaviour. Opting back in, then, may also require *modifying the interface,* not just the behaviour. Tools like *uBlock Origin, Freedom, Indistractable,* or even custom-built RSS dashboards are not patches for digital excess. They are instruments of governance—ways to *reassert authorship over your informational landscape.*

It is also worth noting that selective re-engagement is not an endpoint. It is an ongoing posture—*a practice, not a protocol.* Unlike detoxes, which imply restoration through absence, this practice gains its clarity through presence: through noticing how certain interfaces feel, how certain time blocks perform, how certain interactions affect one's ability to think clearly and act meaningfully. The reward is not mere efficiency. It is *the return of cognitive sovereignty.*

Frameworks help. One useful lens is the idea of *digital cadence*—the rhythm with which one enters and exits digital domains. A journalist may maintain a high-frequency cadence with Twitter during working hours, but a low-frequency one with messaging apps. A researcher may toggle between dense digital reading and offline note synthesis. The cadence is not about consistency—it is about *coherence with goals.* When the rhythm of engagement reflects the rhythm of thought, digital tools become extensions rather than invasions of mental life.

Another framework is *purpose-based partitioning*: separating activities by intent. Is this tool for discovery, for creation, for connection, or for entertainment? When each digital space is attached to a clear purpose, switching between them becomes a meaningful transition—not a blurring of cognitive boundaries. This can be supported by environment design: using different devices, desktops, or even physical locations to cue different modes of attention.

Yet no framework is a substitute for *self-awareness*. The most important tool in selective re-engagement is *discernment*. Not every notification is urgent. Not every platform deserves a reply. Not every silence is a void. And not every form of presence requires visibility. These insights become accessible only through *practice in slowness*, and through a refusal to treat friction as failure. In this context, friction becomes a filter—*a way of honouring your own thresholds*.

This reorientation runs counter to prevailing norms. Popular discourse around tech tends to oscillate between utopianism and alarmism: either we are being liberated by innovation, or we are being hijacked by manipulation. But the truth is more granular. *Most technologies are neither emancipatory nor oppressive by default. They are pliable, shaped by the intentions of their designers and the choices of their users.* Opting back in, then, is an act of subtle resistance—a way of stepping into that grey space with intelligence and care.

Ultimately, the power to re-engage selectively is an expression of maturity. It affirms that agency is not found in isolation from systems, but in wise interaction with them. It accepts that the answer to digital overload is not digital absence, but *digital discernment*. That discernment—earned, not assumed—is what allows us to be *present, not just connected*. In a culture that rewards always-on visibility, choosing when and how to engage is a quiet, sustained form of sovereignty.

Chapter 9
Resistance by Design

Every tap, swipe, and scroll is guided by invisible choices—decisions most users never glimpse, yet which profoundly shape behaviour, thought, and engagement. From the architecture of a mobile app to the defaults baked into a web browser, design is never neutral. It embodies assumptions, favours certain actions, and sidelines others. In a platformed world where attention is currency and friction is framed as failure, opting out is more complicated than it appears. Genuine autonomy, it seems, must be deliberately engineered, not passively assumed. Resistance by design is not about romanticising disconnection or glorifying hacker culture. It is about recognising that the interface is political, and that our capacity for agency increasingly hinges on the systems we consent to—or refuse.

Power today is rarely exercised through overt force. Instead, it operates through defaults. The "share location" prompt, the endless scroll framed as convenience, the glaring "accept all cookies" button beside a muted "manage settings" link—these are not glitches; they are deliberate governance. Design shapes perception, nudges behaviour, and narrows options in subtle, calibrated ways. Navigating this terrain intentionally requires fluency in design politics: to see not just what the interface presents, but what it conceals, privileges, and whose interests it serves.

Yet resistance is not only critique; it is also creation. Across disciplines, technologists, designers, and activists are quietly building alternative infrastructures—ones that prize deliberation over dependence, transparency over obfuscation, autonomy over automation. Platforms such as Signal, Fathom, and Mastodon challenge centralised paradigms by decentralising control, removing tracking, or foregrounding human governance over algorithmic authority. In each, the logic shifts from managing users to respecting them.

This is not nostalgia for an "innocent web." It is a forward-looking approach rooted in a simple truth: the tools we use shape our habits, and our habits shape our lives. Predictive browsers, curated feeds, and prioritised calendars are no longer neutral instruments; they are pedagogy. They train, guide, and influence us at scale, quietly rewriting relevance and priorities. The question is not whether design shapes behaviour, but whether we remain aware of it—whether the systems we build or adopt expand our possibilities or confine them within predetermined bounds.

Resistance, then, is not a dramatic protest; it is thoughtful refusal. It is rejecting invisible norms and replacing them with intentional alternatives. This can be systemic—contributing to open-source tools that counter surveillance capitalism—or personal, such as establishing private protocols for digital engagement. The essence lies not only in what we reject, but in what we choose to enact instead. This chapter follows that trajectory—from critique to creation, from reaction to design.

Designing for autonomy does not mean eliminating structure, but rendering it legible and flexible. Platforms often present choice as a burden, a source of fatigue or disengagement. Real freedom, however, is not absence of constraint; it is intelligent configuration of it. What if interfaces slowed gratification to preserve reflection? What if recommendation engines required users to articulate criteria rather than harvest past behaviour? What if defaults were rooted in consent rather than corporate expedience? These are not utopian ideals—they are the coordinates of a parallel design culture quietly emerging today.

The browser illustrates this frontier vividly. As the gateway to much of the digital world, it wields subtle but profound influence. Mainstream options embed search engines, data collection processes, and interoperability choices that serve corporate interests. Counter-systems like Firefox, Brave, or the experimental Beaker Browser do more than block ads—they rethink how pages are served, identities tracked, and code executed. The browser becomes a contested space: a portal of control, or a platform of permission.

Maps are another critical front. Location services drive advertising, navigation, and behavioural prediction. Google Maps, for instance, optimises not only for efficiency but for monetisation—promoting paying businesses, privileging engagement-maximising routes. OpenStreetMap counters this logic, returning agency to contributors and stripping out monetised distortions. Neutrality is revealed as a fiction; the shaping of space is inseparable from values, incentives, and vision. Resistance here is epistemic as much as geographic.

Perhaps the most neglected site of resistance is the self. Platforms offer toggles, opt-outs, and settings, yet these are reactive and often symbolic. True autonomy begins by rewriting the terms of participation entirely—crafting personal protocols that exist outside platform logic. Checking social media only on a second device, encrypting messages by default, browsing pseudonymously—these are not merely technical acts; they are philosophical ones, affirming that sovereignty originates in self-authorship.

Resistance by design is not anti-technology. It is anti-instrumentalism: a belief that systems should function well, for the right reasons, in service of human values. Properly shaped tools can help us think more clearly, decide more deliberately, and live more responsibly. This stance is moral as much as technical, insisting that designers act as stewards, not enforcers of compliance.

This chapter invites readers to examine power at the level of interface. To see where defaults dictate behaviour, to discern which design choices constrain and which expand freedom. More than critique, it emphasises creation: frameworks for alternative tools, case studies of systems prioritising consent and comprehension, and principles for resisting not the digital realm itself, but the logics that distort it. What emerges is a call not to abandon design, but to reclaim it—to make it a field of ethical innovation.

For those seeking to reclaim digital life, resistance is an ongoing practice. It requires learning how things work, rejecting what fails, and building what might. It begins with clarity: clarity about the world we inhabit, and the world we wish to help bring into being. Design at its best is not seduction; it is intention. The moment has arrived to design not only what we use, but how we use it. This chapter is a blueprint for that endeavour.

Hacking the Defaults

To understand digital power today, one need not look to state surveillance or corporate lobbying alone. Increasingly, influence is encoded in the defaults—the pre-set paths and silent assumptions embedded into the digital tools we use daily. The scroll of a feed, the destination of a map, the suggested search, the notification frequency: all of these reflect design decisions made not in consultation with the user but *for* them, often invisibly. Defaults are not passive conveniences. They are strategic architecture, shaping user behaviour long before consent is asked or choice becomes apparent. In this context, hacking the defaults is not a fringe activity; it is a quiet form of digital resistance—an act of reclaiming one's autonomy from design systems that presume too much.

What makes defaults so powerful is their subtlety. Research in behavioural economics and human-computer interaction has long shown that default settings exert a disproportionate influence on user decisions—not because users actively agree with them, but because they simplify action, reduce friction, and signal trust. A now-classic example is organ donation consent rates in Europe: countries where the default is opt-in have dramatically higher participation than those requiring explicit sign-up, despite near-identical populations and healthcare systems. This "default effect" is amplified online, where the speed of interaction and the illusion of personal control mask how few choices are actually made freely. *To use a platform "as intended" is often to conform unknowingly to someone else's blueprint of engagement.*

It is precisely this power—quiet, scalable, and built into the seams of digital life—that a growing cohort of designers, developers, and activists are challenging. Their work doesn't start with outrage or technophobia. It begins with infrastructure: reimagining the protocols, platforms, and defaults that define digital experience. Consider the rise of alternative browsers like Firefox, Brave, or Vivaldi. Each offers not just a different visual skin but a different set of priorities—privacy over data extraction, user control over algorithmic nudging, customisation over homogeneity. Brave, for example, blocks third-party ads and trackers by default, disrupting the surveillance capitalist model at its root. Firefox, backed by Mozilla, positions itself as a civic actor, embedding tools like Enhanced Tracking Protection and DNS-over-HTTPS to safeguard user rights. These are not just products. They are arguments in code—challenges to the assumption that digital convenience must come at the cost of digital sovereignty.

Beyond browsers, open-source mapping projects like OpenStreetMap (OSM) offer a compelling counter-example to commercial geospatial platforms like Google Maps or Apple Maps. OSM, built by a global community of volunteer mappers, does not rely on behavioural profiling to offer directions or local business suggestions. Its maps are editable, localised, and often more accurate in underrepresented regions. Critically, they are not optimised for commerce. Whereas Google Maps may steer users toward partner businesses or ad-sponsored listings, OSM reflects a geographic commons—a collaborative representation of space not owned by any one company. *By resisting the commercial logic baked into proprietary defaults, OpenStreetMap exemplifies how civic infrastructure can rival corporate incumbents without mirroring their assumptions.*

These counter-systems are not nostalgic retreats into pre-digital simplicity. On the contrary, they are technologically sophisticated, often more transparent and customisable than their mainstream counterparts. Their distinguishing feature is not technical inferiority but political intentionality. Tools like Signal—a privacy-focused messaging app developed by a non-profit—demonstrate this well. Signal offers end-to-end encryption, minimal data collection, and open-source transparency. Crucially, its encryption is the default, not an optional feature hidden behind user settings. This inversion of default logic—from data extraction to data protection—signals a profound shift in what digital design can prioritise when unshackled from ad-based revenue models.

There is a broader philosophical point at stake here. Defaults encode a theory of the user: what they want, how they behave, what they're willing to sacrifice. In most mainstream systems, that theory is economically expedient but epistemologically thin. Users are modelled not as autonomous agents but as predictable input-output machines whose behaviours can be nudged toward profitable outcomes. What happens when tools are built on a different theory of the user—one that assumes curiosity, discernment, and a desire for meaningful control? This is the question that projects like Tails (The Amnesic Incognito Live System), a security-focused operating system used by journalists and activists, attempt to answer. By routing all network traffic through Tor and leaving no digital trace, Tails treats anonymity not as a suspicious exception but as a legitimate starting point for ethical computing. In doing so, it reconfigures the baseline expectations of safety and freedom in digital space.

It is tempting to view such examples as niche outliers, relevant only to privacy maximalists or tech-savvy hobbyists. But this would be a mistake. Many of these tools—while initially adopted by more technically inclined users—serve as bellwethers for broader shifts in public expectation. Just as Firefox helped normalise tabbed browsing and ad blockers before Chrome adopted similar features, so too do today's counter-systems push the Overton window of what is considered normal, possible, or desirable in digital design. *Hacking the defaults is not merely about switching tools; it is about altering the trajectory of design norms themselves.*

The political implications are significant. Every interface carries implicit power relations: what can be seen, what can be done, and what remains out of reach. Defaults act as gatekeepers to that power, funnelling users toward certain behaviours while rendering others invisible or laborious. Thus, to change the defaults is to engage in interface politics—a form of activism that operates not through protest slogans but through pixels, configurations, and protocols. This has led to new forms of design literacy, where understanding interface choices becomes as important as reading terms of service. Projects like Tactical Tech's Data Detox Kit or the Digital Rights Foundation's security guides exemplify this trend, offering non-technical users ways to rethink how they engage with platforms—how to change what is presumed, not just what is permitted.

Yet this is not a simple call to "opt out." Total disengagement from mainstream platforms is neither practical nor necessarily desirable. The value of hacking the defaults lies not in purism but in pluralism: making room for a broader ecosystem of tools that respect user agency, encourage deliberation, and challenge extractive models of engagement. It is about creating—and sustaining—an architecture of alternatives. This requires not just better tools but better infrastructures: funding models that support open-source sustainability, legal frameworks that mandate interoperability, and educational efforts that build digital discernment into civic literacy. *Without systemic support, even the most principled tools remain precarious—dependent on volunteer labour, patchwork funding, and the goodwill of a small community.*

Still, there are grounds for cautious optimism. The resurgence of interest in decentralised platforms like Mastodon, the growing visibility of ethical tech certification projects, and the renewed push for regulation of dark patterns all point to a climate more attuned to the politics of design. It is increasingly understood that software is not neutral, and that choice architecture matters as much as codebase efficiency. In this context, hacking the defaults is less about sabotage than stewardship—a careful effort to reorient the digital environment toward human flourishing rather than passive compliance.

If the past decade has taught us anything, it is that convenience comes with a cost. The defaults that promise seamlessness often smuggle in assumptions about identity, behaviour, and value that deserve scrutiny. Fortunately, the tools to contest those defaults—however imperfect—are within reach. To choose them is not merely to switch software. It is to take a stand, however quietly, for a different kind of digital life—one where choice is not just available, but intelligible and meaningful.

The Politics of Interface

Every interface is an argument. Whether it's the seamless glide of a checkout button, the absence of a "dislike" option, or the frictionless pull-to-refresh gesture that mimics a slot machine lever, digital environments embed choices not only about what users can do, but what they are encouraged—or discouraged—to think, feel, and become. These are not neutral design decisions. They are the front lines of modern governance, enacted not by elected officials but by engineers, designers, and product teams whose choices now shape cognition at scale. When interfaces become the grammar of everyday interaction, their defaults become doctrine.

That doctrine is rarely transparent. Consider the interface of a mainstream social platform. At first glance, it appears to offer freedom: an empty status box, a responsive feed, a search bar awaiting your intent. But under the surface lies a complex choreography of engineered nudges—ranking algorithms that dictate which friends appear most often, notifications that prioritise engagement over relevance, and input fields that constrain emotional expression to a palette of predefined reactions. What looks like design elegance is often a scaffold for subtle control. The interface doesn't just serve the user; it serves the platform's underlying incentives—often tied to monetisation, retention, and behavioural prediction.

Power, in the age of interfaces, is exercised through structure, not command. The absence of a clear path is a message. So is the presence of only two options when three are needed. Every omission and every default is a design statement—one that often goes unscrutinised because of the false assumption that "user-friendly" is synonymous with "user-controlled." But design is never value-free. It always encodes a perspective on what is important, who is in control, and what kind of world is being made possible.

This is especially evident in the politics of consent. Consider the typical cookie pop-up in Europe. While regulatory compliance demands that platforms obtain informed consent for data tracking, most designs bury the "reject all" option under layers of friction—small text, extra clicks, or confusing toggles—while highlighting the "accept all" with visual ease. The message is clear: compliance is performative; consent is coerced. The user interface becomes an instrument not of empowerment, but of strategic obfuscation.

A similar dynamic plays out in app onboarding flows. When users sign up for a service, the defaults are often pre-selected: newsletter subscriptions, data sharing preferences, or facial recognition settings are "opt-out" rather than "opt-in." Each clickstream is shaped to guide the user toward the company's preferred outcome. This is not accidental. It is *architectural influence*—a mode of governance that hides in plain sight, enacted not through ideology but interface.

The ramifications extend far beyond convenience or annoyance. Interfaces mediate access to knowledge, resources, relationships, and even selfhood. When a platform's design privileges visibility based on conformity to a particular aesthetic—say, filtered beauty or attention-grabbing outrage—it is no longer merely organising content; it is setting cultural norms. The interface becomes a political actor, shaping whose voices are heard, whose identities are legible, and which forms of presence are rewarded. Visibility, in this sense, is power—and it is negotiated pixel by pixel.

Nowhere is this more evident than in the feedback systems that underpin social media platforms. The like button, for instance, may seem like an innocuous tool for connection. But it also reconfigures social approval into a metric—encouraging quantifiable popularity over qualitative nuance. This shift affects not just content production, but user psychology: individuals begin to optimise their behaviour for platform affirmation, a process that transforms personal expression into algorithmic performance. What is rewarded gets repeated, and soon the interface becomes a mirror, reflecting not who we are, but what the platform prefers us to be.

This is not an argument against all interface design. Rather, it is a call to examine its premises and politics. Because every tool, however elegant, has affordances and constraints. A search engine that auto-completes questions differently based on geolocation or prior searches is not simply predictive—it is prescriptive. A dating app that allows only binary gender choices is not just limited—it is exclusionary. A news app that disables comments under certain stories is not just moderating—it is curating discourse. These choices are all political—not in the partisan sense, but in their implications for agency, representation, and power.

The concept of "affordance" in design theory—coined by psychologist James J. Gibson and later applied to human-computer interaction—describes the actionable possibilities that an object or environment offers. A door handle affords pulling; a button affords pressing. But digital interfaces also afford ideologies. A swipe, a nudge, a modal dialogue box—all can encode assumptions about user behaviour, values, and acceptable outcomes. These affordances are often culturally specific, and their power lies precisely in their invisibility.

Designers and technologists increasingly recognise this. There is a growing movement—sometimes called "design justice"—that argues for more inclusive, equitable, and transparent design practices. It calls attention to the fact that marginalised communities often encounter interfaces not as tools, but as barriers: automated job portals that discard non-traditional CVs, facial recognition software that fails on darker skin tones, biometric systems that presume a singular body norm. These are not edge cases; they are design failures with political consequences.

To challenge the politics of interface is not to demand ideological neutrality, but to foreground intentionality. Platforms must ask: Whose needs are centred? Whose labour is obscured? Whose autonomy is traded for efficiency? These are not design questions alone; they are ethical ones. And they require interdisciplinary thinking—drawing from philosophy, sociology, and critical race theory, not just UX heuristics and A/B tests.

Some designers respond to this challenge by creating counter-interfaces—tools that deliberately introduce friction or transparency to disrupt default behaviours. The "Are You Sure?" plugin, which asks users to rephrase toxic tweets before sending, slows down aggression by design. Browsers like Brave or extensions like uBlock Origin reject the advertising-centric business model entirely, prioritising user control over corporate surveillance. These tools may lack the polish of mainstream platforms, but they offer something far rarer: ideological clarity.

Still, meaningful change cannot rely on individual tools alone. It demands a shift in mindset—from "ease of use" to "depth of use." From maximising clicks to maximising comprehension. From hiding complexity to designing for it. The politics of interface are not resolved through better onboarding or colour palettes; they are resolved through sustained critique, participatory design, and structural accountability.

Ultimately, to interface is to interact. And interaction is never neutral. The interfaces we use daily are not just portals to information; they are maps of power. They tell us what is possible, what is permissible, and what is preferred. To understand them deeply—to read them as texts, as architectures, as arguments—is not a matter of technical literacy. It is a matter of civic literacy. In a world increasingly run by platforms, our freedom is not defined only by what we can say, but by how we are allowed to say it—and whether we are even heard at all.

Building for Choice, Not Control

Design, once a discipline rooted in aesthetics and usability, has grown into one of the most consequential instruments of power in the digital age. Every interface element, from the placement of a button to the frictionless swipe of a feed, exerts force—either gently guiding or aggressively corralling user behaviour. The tools we use are not neutral platforms; they are frameworks embedded with assumptions, incentives, and constraints. Increasingly, these frameworks are designed to predict, direct, and monetise our decisions, not to foster free expression or thoughtful choice. The very technologies once hailed as engines of empowerment now often operate as architectures of subtle control. To reverse this trajectory, we must turn our attention to the art—and politics—of designing for choice rather than control.

This distinction is more than a philosophical posture. It has real consequences. A platform designed to enhance autonomy seeks to expand the field of possible actions a user might take, while one designed to maximise control narrows that field to optimise for behavioural predictability. Take the example of search engine auto-suggestions. A benign feature on the surface, they often shape what people *intend* to search before the thought is fully formed. Predictive algorithms gently herd users toward commercially or socially dominant narratives, favouring visibility over variety, speed over depth. Designing for choice means resisting that gravitational pull and allowing cognitive space for reflection—even at the cost of immediate engagement.

Building for autonomy requires rethinking many core assumptions in mainstream UX and product development. Designers are typically rewarded for reducing friction, streamlining interaction, and nudging users toward intended outcomes. These are metrics of efficiency, not agency. But ease is not always the ally of freedom. Systems that *encourage pause*—whether through subtle time delays, confirmation prompts, or thoughtful configuration options—may lower conversion rates but raise the quality of the user's decision-making. For example, the note-taking app Obsidian prioritises user sovereignty through local storage and plugin modularity, allowing individuals to shape their workflows without data lock-in or imposed hierarchies. By contrast, Google Docs, while undeniably more accessible, subtly defaults users into cloud storage, live collaboration, and Google's ecosystem-wide telemetry.

The tension is not binary—it's architectural. A calendar app, for instance, can be designed to prioritise user-defined boundaries (such as blocking time for deep work) or to serve as a scheduling sponge that optimises for availability to others. Both interfaces offer similar functions but encode radically different assumptions about time, agency, and attention. This is why genuine autonomy cannot be restored through a simple toggle or dashboard setting. It must be built into the logic of the system itself. Choice isn't merely the presence of multiple options; it is the capacity to *meaningfully evaluate and act upon* them.

This point is often lost in mainstream discussions of "user control," which tend to confuse configurability with autonomy. A highly customisable app might still enforce manipulative defaults or track behaviour across sessions without meaningful consent. True autonomy rests not in how many knobs users can turn but in whether they can orient their actions in alignment with their values—without coercion, obfuscation, or artificial constraint. A more honest design philosophy starts by interrogating who benefits from a given interface's choices. When Uber hides surge pricing behind small icons, or Spotify auto-plays algorithmic playlists instead of album tracks, they are making powerfully normative claims about what the user *should* want—even if that claim is masked as convenience.

Some designers and developers are actively pushing against these paradigms. The open-source community surrounding tools like Mastodon or Signal offers illuminating counter-examples. These projects are not merely "alternatives"—they are assertions of different priorities. Signal, for instance, refuses to compromise on end-to-end encryption, even at the expense of user onboarding speed. Mastodon disperses identity and moderation authority across decentralised servers, preserving individual autonomy over centralised convenience. These are not market decisions—they are design ideologies. They reflect an understanding that *freedom is a product of structure, not its absence.*

Yet the challenge is not just in building tools with better ethical scaffolding. It's also about cultivating design cultures that embrace restraint. The impulse to solve every problem with a dashboard, badge, or behavioural nudge can lead to experiences that are over-designed but under-liberating. A genuinely empowering interface is often quieter, more patient. It might ask more of the user—not less—and in doing so, provide the space for more meaningful interaction. Take the example of the writing tool Drafts, which foregrounds minimalism and delay. It doesn't assume the destination for your words, allowing you to export, share, or delete only when you're ready. Such friction, far from being a flaw, becomes a feature that protects deliberation.

Designing for autonomy also invites a reassessment of metrics. Most tech companies rely on KPIs like time-on-site, click-through rate, or user retention—all proxies for stickiness, not sovereignty. A tool built for choice must be evaluated through a different lens: Did it help the user act with intention? Did it allow them to express a value, boundary, or preference that might otherwise have been overwritten by system logic? These are harder questions to measure—but they are the right ones to ask. Because a platform that optimises for autonomy may, paradoxically, encourage less use, not more. And in that reduction, it may offer something closer to real value.

There are, of course, trade-offs. Autonomy-friendly tools often involve steeper learning curves, reduced interoperability, or diminished economies of scale. They may be slower, more fragmented, or less intuitive at first glance. But they reward effort with integrity. A password manager that stores data locally may not offer seamless syncing across devices—but it grants users sole control over their credentials. A browser that blocks third-party cookies by default might deliver less targeted content—but it limits surveillance by design, not as an afterthought. In both cases, the inconvenience is a cost of freedom, not a failure of usability.

Designing for choice also means recognising the structural asymmetries between users and platforms. Most users operate within systems they did not choose, under terms they did not negotiate, governed by incentives they do not understand. Rebalancing this asymmetry requires *not* just more granular settings or ethical charters, but a reconfiguration of where interpretive authority lies. Giving users the ability to read logs of data collected, access granular permission controls, or port their data to another platform are all steps toward epistemic parity—bridging the knowledge gap that allows control to masquerade as care.

Ultimately, the future of user autonomy depends not on nostalgia for an imagined "open web," but on the active creation of alternatives that honour complexity without coercion. To design for choice is not to abandon guidance or intentionality, but to foreground them transparently, with accountability and respect. It is to build tools that trust users to navigate ambiguity, to wrestle with competing impulses, to sometimes make inefficient or unpopular decisions—and to do so with dignity intact.

Control may be profitable, but choice is principled. And in the long run, principled systems are the ones that endure—not because they capture attention, but because they deserve it.

Personal Protocols for Digital Sovereignty

The myth of seamless convenience has seduced much of the modern world into a passive relationship with technology. With each opt-in, pre-checked box, and algorithmically tailored feed, our digital lives have become optimised not for personal values or discernment but for ease, engagement, and efficiency. But ease has a cost: the quiet erosion of self-direction. In a system that rarely asks what we want—only what we'll click—*digital sovereignty* becomes less a given and more a practice. A personal protocol is precisely that: a deliberately designed set of behavioural and cognitive commitments that empower individuals to reclaim control without having to fully unplug.

Most mainstream technology encourages outsourcing decision-making. Default privacy settings on social platforms, auto-play on video services, personalised ad recommendations, and dark pattern design all guide behaviour subtly yet pervasively. Few users pause to rewrite these scripts. And even fewer develop a personal philosophy robust enough to govern how, when, and why they engage with the digital sphere. The result is an ecosystem where the architecture of control is invisible but deeply embedded—one in which opting out feels extreme, and opting in by default is the only convenient choice.

To craft a personal protocol for digital sovereignty is to reverse this logic—to design one's own interface with the digital world deliberately, reflexively, and resiliently.

This requires more than adjusting settings. It means recognising that true agency isn't toggled by platform features but established through intentional habits and internal commitments. Consider someone who decides to check email only twice a day. This choice runs counter to the push-notification culture of immediacy, but it signals a different allegiance: attention over urgency. Or think of individuals who refuse to consume news via algorithmic curation, choosing instead a set of curated sources checked weekly. These aren't just lifestyle tweaks; they are *values in motion*—protocols that surface deeply held beliefs about time, truth, and trust.

Importantly, such practices cannot be standardised. What constitutes digital sovereignty for a political journalist may look very different for a clinical researcher, artist, or parent. For some, it might involve blocking addictive sites during creative work hours. For others, it might mean maintaining strict boundaries between professional and personal communication channels. The core principle is the same: *consciously shape the rules of engagement rather than inheriting those of the platform.*

Historically, systems of governance—whether political or technological—have relied on an implicit assumption: the average person lacks the time, literacy, or motivation to self-regulate meaningfully. This assumption has produced interfaces that flatter us with surface choices while quietly enclosing the terrain of deeper decision-making. Personal protocols reject this passivity. They posit that, given thoughtful guidance and reflective space, people are capable of designing behavioural contracts more ethical, responsive, and effective than any terms-of-service agreement ever drafted.

The idea of a "personal protocol" owes a debt to movements in digital minimalism, cybersecurity hygiene, and behavioural design. But unlike digital detoxes or one-size-fits-all tech manifestos, protocols are context-sensitive, modular, and adaptive. They are frameworks rather than commandments. What matters is not ideological purity but pragmatic fit: does this practice serve your values, priorities, and limits? Can it evolve with your changing relationship to technology?

This fluidity is essential. Unlike traditional laws or externally imposed constraints, personal protocols work because they are *chosen*, not mandated. They invite self-awareness rather than compliance. Consider the case of open-source developers who log every plugin and extension they use—not to signal virtue, but to maintain transparency over their digital dependencies. Or privacy-conscious users who maintain multiple browser profiles segmented by identity: one for research, one for socialising, one for anonymous browsing. These structures don't arise from default settings; they emerge from reflective experimentation, iterated over time.

It is tempting to believe that platforms will eventually become more humane, more aligned with user autonomy. And there is reason for cautious optimism—emerging movements in ethical UX, data rights legislation, and humane tech design do point in this direction. But to wait for systemic reform is to delay personal responsibility. In the meantime, it is both possible and necessary to develop independent governance strategies. *Just as democracies require civic participation to thrive, digital systems require intentional users to stay ethical.*

This perspective complicates the notion of freedom. Most of us were taught to think of freedom as the absence of constraint—freedom from. But digital sovereignty increasingly means *freedom through structure*. The right constraints, chosen deliberately, protect us from coercive design. They anchor us when frictionless systems would pull us under. In this sense, personal protocols are a form of modern self-discipline—not in the puritanical sense, but in the stoic sense: a refusal to be mastered by invisible architectures.

Frameworks for developing such protocols can draw inspiration from diverse sources. Behavioural psychology highlights the power of pre-commitment devices—tools that help people stick to their intentions, such as content blockers or screen time quotas. Cognitive science offers models for managing attention, like the Pomodoro technique or mindful context-switching. Philosophy, particularly from traditions such as existentialism and virtue ethics, reminds us that autonomy isn't just about what we do, but how deliberately we do it.

Still, no single framework suffices. Individuals must construct systems that are both principled and elastic. This might mean identifying core digital values (e.g. privacy, focus, informational integrity), mapping which platforms support or undermine them, and developing a layered response: technical tools, behavioural routines, and reflective checkpoints. A user might block attention-hijacking sites during writing hours, maintain a personal data audit log monthly, and schedule quarterly "tech reviews" to adjust habits based on life changes. These are not corporate settings or app features—they are *acts of digital citizenship*, privately enacted but publicly consequential.

Critically, personal protocols are not anti-technology. They are anti-passivity. They do not require that users abandon tools, but that they interrogate them. They are not about control for its own sake, but about crafting a coherent relationship between digital environments and lived priorities. *The goal is not to escape the feed, but to shape how, when, and why one enters it.*

As systems grow more complex and algorithmic mediation becomes the norm, the burden of discernment shifts further to the individual. In such a landscape, the ability to craft and revise one's own digital protocols may become as essential as budgeting or basic health literacy. These habits cannot be outsourced. They must be designed, maintained, and internalised—not just to survive in the digital age, but to live meaningfully within it.

Ultimately, personal protocols do not promise control over the digital world. They promise coherence within it. And in an age increasingly defined by behavioural automation and ambient surveillance, that coherence is not just a luxury—it is a form of resistance. Thoughtfully structured, deliberately enacted, and continually revised, *these user-defined contracts are perhaps the most vital tool we have for reclaiming authorship of our digital lives.*

Chapter 10
Knowing When You're Choosing

Modern life is awash with choices, yet the sheer number we face often obscures a more unsettling reality: many of them aren't truly ours. Digital interfaces are designed to feel empowering—sliders, toggles, personalised feeds, endless scrolls "tailored for you." Yet behavioural research and lived experience alike suggest that what we call autonomy is often little more than a performance of freedom. Defaults, nudges, recommendation engines, and systemic constraints operate beneath our awareness. And if we cannot perceive the frame in which a choice occurs, can we really claim authorship over it?

This chapter begins by confronting a deceptively simple question: how can we tell when we are genuinely choosing? Not simply clicking or typing, but acting from deliberate intent rather than a defaulted path. To answer this, we need sharper conceptual tools. One approach is the "Test for Intentionality"—a framework to parse whether a decision arises from reflection or from convenience, habit, or algorithmic suggestion. It does not produce binary answers but prompts scrutiny: which alternatives did I consider? Which constraints did I inherit? Which assumptions am I operating under?

The illusion of choice is most seductive when technological environments anticipate our preferences and smooth our actions. Yet streamlining is never neutral. Every platform setting embodies a politics, every interface a set of values. Did you choose that meal, or was it recommended based on previous orders? Did you select the article, or did an algorithm push it into your feed? When probabilistic models optimise for attention, the appearance of choice can become manipulation, in which engagement masks extraction.

To navigate these complexities, this chapter introduces a framework of three levels of agency: choice of the system, choice within the system, and choice about the system. Most users operate at the middle layer—interacting with menus, adjusting preferences, moving within boundaries set by others. Far fewer question the first or third layers: whether the system itself is appropriate to use, and what its participation implies for values, attention, or relationships. Transitioning from interface literacy to infrastructural awareness restores a deeper sovereignty, one that encompasses both micro-decisions and meta-decisions—the ability to define the terrain itself.

These concerns are not abstract. Few people meaningfully switch search engines, email providers, or cloud services, despite alternatives. Such habits are rarely conscious endorsements; they are habituated convenience. Smart assistants, predictive keyboards, and auto-complete features promise efficiency but exact an epistemic toll: the more we let systems finish our thoughts, the less conscious we become of how those thoughts are shaped. Efficiency becomes the enemy of awareness. By default, we follow the path of least resistance, surrendering in subtle increments our capacity to notice, reflect, and reframe.

Yet withdrawal is not the answer. Complete disconnection is neither desirable nor sustainable in digitised economies. What is required is engaged awareness: inhabiting designed systems while remaining critically attuned to how they condition behaviour. This is not paranoia nor Luddism; it is design literacy fused with moral discernment—a way of navigating digital environments without being quietly reprogrammed by them.

Promising practices are emerging from fields as varied as user experience design, philosophy of technology, behavioural economics, and digital ethics. Some designers are experimenting with friction as a feature, not a bug—requiring users to pause before sharing, to retype rather than retweet, to reflect before reacting. Others visualise the costs of choices: the time spent, the data harvested, the behavioural patterns reinforced. These tools do not presume omniscience or perfect rationality, but they respect the user enough to render the architecture visible, supporting reflection rather than silently steering action.

The imperative for awareness will only intensify as digital systems grow more pervasive. Ambient computing, emotion-sensing devices, AI companions, and persistent personalisation promise unprecedented convenience—but they also challenge the very notion of autonomous agency. When a device completes your sentences, schedules your meetings, plays music to shape mood, and offers companionship tailored to your psychological profile, what does choosing even mean? What does resisting mean? And what, if anything, remains unmediated?

The final section of this chapter addresses these questions strategically, offering conceptual tools and practical habits to safeguard agency. Autonomy does not require isolation; it requires discernment within connection. It is not about opting out entirely but cultivating the literacy and courage to opt in deliberately.

True autonomy is not a fixed trait; it is a muscle, honed and strengthened over time. Recognising when we are choosing is an ongoing discipline: tracing the origins of our preferences, distinguishing those that serve us from those imposed without consent, and inserting pauses, interruptions, and questions into routines.

Above all, it is about reclaiming authorship—not merely over actions, but over the context in which they unfold. In a world engineered to anticipate us, the act of noticing before acting—the conscious awareness that a choice is truly ours—may be the most radical act of all.

The Test for Intentionality

Most people believe they are making choices, when in fact they are selecting from options already designed for them. Whether accepting a recommended show, allowing default tracking settings, or clicking the first search result, the sensation of decision-making often masks the quiet guidance of underlying architectures. *Intentionality is not merely about having options—it is about recognising the context that produced them.* To reclaim genuine agency in digital environments, one must go beyond the surface of interface and begin interrogating the subtle scripts running beneath. That process begins with asking a deceptively difficult question: was this decision truly mine?

Understanding the difference between a decision made and a decision inherited is now a critical skill. Yet digital systems are not neutral arenas of possibility—they are preconditioned spaces optimised for business metrics:

engagement, retention, monetisation. The interface becomes a script, encouraging one kind of behaviour over another. In this landscape, the mental model known as *The Test for Intentionality* serves as a practical and philosophical tool for assessing the authenticity of our choices. It invites users to pause, examine, and articulate the origin of their actions—not only what they chose, but *why* they chose it, and what forces shaped that path.

A functional version of this test has three components: awareness, alternative, and authorship. The first layer, awareness, asks whether the decision was made in a state of conscious attention. Were you present, reflective, and aware of the moment of choice—or were you responding automatically to a prompt, notification, or habit loop? Consider how many people open social media reflexively, not out of deliberate intent but conditioned response. Awareness is the precursor to freedom. *Without attention, there is no agency—only momentum.*

The second layer, alternative, probes whether meaningful options were visible and accessible at the time. If every button leads to the same destination, if dissent is buried three clicks deep, if the interface discourages exploration—then the appearance of choice is a veneer. An example can be seen in cookie consent banners: one button says "Accept All," bright and central. The path to granular settings is smaller, less visible, sometimes designed to frustrate. Technically, the user consents—but substantively, the system funnels them into conformity. *A choice that requires disproportionate effort to enact is not a real choice—it's a performance of compliance.*

The third layer, authorship, asks a more intimate question: does this decision reflect your values, goals, or needs—or someone else's? This is the domain of identity, not just behaviour. Choosing a news source, joining a platform, or sharing content may feel spontaneous, but it is often an echo of social pressure, recommendation systems, or pre-established patterns. Authorship means being able to trace the origins of a decision to a coherent sense of self, rather than a reactive cascade triggered by design. It is what separates a user from a user profile.

When all three layers—awareness, alternative, and authorship—are present, one can reasonably say a choice is intentional. But in digital contexts, one or more of these layers is routinely compromised. That's not accidental. Modern platforms are explicitly built to reduce friction, accelerate interaction, and pre-empt user decisions. Consider Netflix's autoplay feature, which begins the next episode before you've consciously decided to watch it. The system removes the space for deliberation, turning a potential decision into an assumed continuation. Or take Amazon's "Buy Now" button—engineered to eliminate the pause that might accompany a traditional checkout process. *Convenience becomes coercion when it removes the chance to think.*

Some might argue that streamlined interfaces are simply efficient—that users don't want to evaluate every click. This is partially true. Not every decision requires existential depth. But the trouble begins when the sum of small, unconscious actions leads to large-scale patterns: a calendar filled with obligations you didn't choose, a feed curated to reinforce bias, a digital identity crafted by your interactions rather than your intentions. Over time, *the erosion of micro-agency compounds into macro-drift*. You find yourself in a life that feels chosen, but in retrospect was merely followed.

There are disciplines that train for this kind of discernment. Philosophers refer to "second-order desires"—not just wanting something, but wanting to want it. The intentional person is not merely reacting to stimuli, but evaluating whether their reactions align with their deeper commitments. Similarly, Buddhist teachings emphasise the difference between impulse and intention. A thought may arise, but the mindful practitioner chooses which ones to feed. The Test for Intentionality shares this ethical ambition: to help people step out of the loop of automaticity and into the space of reflection.

Tools can support this shift. Some designers are building features that insert friction deliberately. The browser extension "Unplug" prompts users before opening specified distracting sites, asking whether the visit is purposeful. Others, like the "Moment" app, visualise time spent on devices and invite users to set mindful limits. These interventions don't eliminate choice—they surface it. *When a system makes you ask, "Is this what I want?"—it is doing more than serving a function; it is supporting a value.*

The same principle can be applied organisationally. In workplace software, for instance, default calendar settings often prioritise availability over focus. Back-to-back meetings become the norm not because people prefer them, but because the tool makes it easy. Changing this requires both technological redesign and cultural awareness: building in breaks, highlighting focus time, reducing meeting length by default. These are small changes, but they create an environment where *decisions are made with intention, not inheritance.*

Still, a test is only useful if it's used. The broader project of reclaiming agency depends not only on conceptual clarity but on practical discipline. Users must cultivate the habit of questioning defaults. They must pause before consenting, reflect before posting, and occasionally invert the platform's logic entirely. This might mean turning off autoplay, switching to alternative apps, or even scripting personal protocols that override interface norms. *It is not enough to wait for better tools. One must become a more intentional user of the tools already available.*

None of this is easy. Intentionality is costly. It demands time, energy, and vigilance—resources already under siege. But the alternative is to outsource selfhood to systems optimised for something else. If we are not careful, we become the sum of our clicks. The Test for Intentionality is not a cure, but a compass. It points us back to ourselves—to our reasons, our rhythms, our right to define what matters.

Ultimately, the goal is not perfect deliberation. It is not about micromanaging every decision or rejecting every suggestion. It is about knowing when a choice reflects your mind, and when it's been manufactured for you. In an age of invisible nudges and engineered defaults, *knowing when you are choosing is the first act of digital sovereignty*. And that, perhaps, is the most meaningful choice you can make.

Three Layers of Choice

It is tempting to view choice as a single act—an isolated moment of preference: selecting a brand, tapping a button, switching a setting. But beneath each of these gestures lies a broader architecture, one in which choice is rarely neutral, and never detached from context. *To fully understand agency in digital environments, we must move beyond the surface of what is chosen and examine the layers that scaffold the act itself.* In contemporary design systems—whether in apps, platforms, or infrastructures—agency unfolds not at one level, but across three: the choice of a system, the choice within it, and the choice about its structure and influence. This framework—*choice of, within, and about*—helps illuminate the real scope of autonomy and, more critically, its limits.

Start with the first and most visible: choice within the system. This is the form of agency users most commonly experience. It includes picking a profile photo, deciding which message to reply to, or choosing between a vegan recipe and a chicken stir fry in a meal-planning app. These are actions bounded by the system's structure and sanctioned by its design. While they may feel personal, creative, or even empowering, they are in fact preconditioned—shaped by the underlying affordances and constraints the system permits. In interface design, this is sometimes referred to as *bounded choice* or *guided interaction*. The system says: "Here are your options. Choose freely—*among these*."

An illustrative example is found in streaming platforms like Spotify or Netflix. The user navigates menus, selects playlists, and chooses genres. Yet all of this occurs within a recommendation engine optimised for engagement, not exploration. The platform does not show all possible options—it shows *what it predicts you will select*. In doing so, it creates an echo chamber of taste, subtly reinforcing what you've liked before, nudging you towards similar content. The freedom to choose within is real—but narrow. *You may pick your path, but the map is drawn by someone else.*

The second layer, choice of the system, is where deeper agency begins. This concerns the selection of the tool, platform, or environment itself. Choosing to use Signal instead of WhatsApp, Firefox instead of Chrome, or ProtonMail instead of Gmail—these are acts of system-level selection. They often reflect a more deliberate stance: a concern for privacy, a desire for open-source alternatives, a refusal to participate in particular data economies. This layer introduces a critical axis—*choice of context*. It acknowledges that not all digital environments are created equal, and that the architecture in which one acts can shape what is possible, permissible, or probable.

However, the choice of the system is frequently obscured. Platforms work hard to establish default dominance. Most users do not select Google Search; they inherit it as a browser default. They do not weigh the merits of iOS over Android with a values-based rubric; they continue with what came bundled in their device. *Network effects, social pressure, and habitual convenience conspire to make switching rare and costly.* In practice, this means that even when better-aligned systems exist—ones with more respectful data policies or more transparent algorithms—most people never reach the threshold of decision. The cost of disruption outweighs the appeal of autonomy.

The final and most profound layer is choice about the system. This involves the capacity to question, reshape, or reject the logics and assumptions embedded in digital infrastructures. It is not just about selecting different tools, but asking *why* the tools work the way they do. Why does the social media timeline sort posts algorithmically rather than chronologically? Why do navigation apps always optimise for speed rather than scenic value, environmental impact, or pedestrian safety? Why are "accept all" options more visible than granular controls in data permissions? *These are not technical inevitabilities—they are design decisions, often made by teams with specific incentives and assumptions.*

Choice about the system includes the possibility of refusal, resistance, or reconfiguration. It is expressed by developers who build alternative infrastructures—like Mastodon or the InterPlanetary File System. It is exercised by regulators who legislate against dark patterns or mandate data portability. And it is embodied by users who set personal protocols: blocking addictive apps, anonymising browsing, or using sandboxed environments to limit exposure. At this level, agency becomes structural—concerned not only with action, but with *the conditions under which action becomes possible.*

One way to visualise the relationship among these three layers is through concentric circles. The innermost ring is *choice within*—fast, frequent, often habitual. The middle is *choice of*—slower, rarer, but more consequential. And the outermost ring is *choice about*—the least accessible, but the most transformative. Most interface design is content to operate within the inner ring. Some forward-thinking systems attempt to support the middle. Very few even acknowledge the outermost.

This matters because the health of one's autonomy depends on the ability to move between these layers fluently. A user may enjoy robust choices within a system but be entirely unaware of better-aligned systems they could adopt. They may pride themselves on choosing the most ethical app, but never question how the app defines what is ethical. Without a broader literacy of system-level design, *agency is often confined to tactical manoeuvres within strategic constraints*. It is like being offered a menu in a restaurant where you cannot see the kitchen, speak to the chef, or influence the sourcing of ingredients.

The framework of three-layered choice is not just diagnostic—it is aspirational. It offers users a way to interrogate their own behaviours, and designers a way to assess how their tools distribute power. For example, an email client that lets users choose themes and folder structures may score well on the "within" layer. One that lets users self-host, export data, and write extensions empowers "choice of." But only if the client also reveals its assumptions—about sorting algorithms, data retention, or integration with surveillance-driven platforms—does it support "choice about."

This layered model also aligns with broader political and philosophical theories of agency. In legal theory, rights are often divided into *positive* and *negative* freedoms—freedom to act versus freedom from coercion. In moral philosophy, thinkers like Isaiah Berlin and Charles Taylor have drawn distinctions between surface preferences and higher-order desires. In the context of digital life, the parallel is clear: *true autonomy requires not only the ability to choose, but the capacity to choose the conditions under which choice becomes meaningful.*

Educational systems that teach digital literacy must move beyond surface-level tutorials. Knowing how to use a platform is no longer enough. Learners need frameworks for assessing which platforms to use and why. They must be able to interrogate incentives, inspect defaults, and trace consequences. *The literacy of agency is not only about competence—it is about consciousness.*

Critics may argue that the complexity of these layers makes the exercise impractical. That users have limited time, that cognitive overload is real, that design must meet people where they are. All true. But meeting people where they are should not mean keeping them there. Just as ethical healthcare balances informed consent with expert guidance, so should digital systems cultivate environments that support deeper awareness over time. *Convenience is not a substitute for empowerment.*

There are signs of progress. Movements for ethical tech, data sovereignty, and user-centred design have begun to operationalise these insights. Projects like Solid (by Tim Berners-Lee) aim to separate data storage from applications, enabling greater choice *about* who controls your information. Platforms like Are.na offer structured yet non-extractive modes of content curation—supporting deliberate engagement *within* an environment that respects context. And services like Fairphone, which let users repair and reconfigure their own devices, exemplify choice *of* a system built around sustainability rather than disposability.

Ultimately, the framework of three layers of choice is not a checklist but a mindset. It invites users to move from passive interaction to conscious navigation. It challenges designers to account not just for usability, but for responsibility. And it urges institutions to think beyond compliance, towards cultures of deliberation. *To live well in designed systems, one must not only act, but know the terrain in which action unfolds.*

By recognising where a choice is happening—within, of, or about—we gain a richer vocabulary for understanding what freedom looks like, and what it demands. In a digital age where attention is harvested, defaults are sticky, and infrastructures are opaque, *asking "where is this choice located?" is not a theoretical exercise—it is a prerequisite for reclaiming agency.*

Living with Designed Systems—Consciously

A user scrolling through a feed is not simply engaging with content—they are navigating an architecture. Every swipe, click, or hesitation feeds a system designed not just to respond to preferences, but to shape them. The idea that digital environments are neutral canvases is both inaccurate and dangerously outdated. Modern interfaces do not merely offer choices; they configure them. They embed assumptions, incentivise certain actions, and render others invisible. To live inside these environments without awareness is to forfeit a measure of agency. Yet opting out entirely is not only impractical—it risks misunderstanding the terrain altogether. The more pressing question is how to inhabit designed systems with discernment, not denial.

The architecture of the digital world operates through affordances—subtle cues about what actions are possible, encouraged, or frictionless. A 'Like' button foregrounds affirmation; the absence of a 'Disagree' or 'Question' button compresses nuance. Infinite scroll removes the natural stopping cues that physical contexts once provided. Algorithms quietly reorder priorities by determining what is surfaced and when. Each design decision—colours, timing, placements, labels—carries political and psychological consequences. These systems don't just support behaviour; they *scaffold it*. They shift the default conditions of attention, interaction, and even belief.

This makes the popular call to 'unplug' or 'detox' feel increasingly insufficient. To withdraw from technology entirely would be to cede the tools of communication, culture, commerce, and governance. A more mature posture is not exit, but reorientation. The challenge is to remain *in* these systems while recognising their shaping force. Conscious digital living begins with understanding that interfaces are arguments. Each presents a view of the world—what matters, what counts, what should happen next. To use them wisely is to engage in ongoing interpretation: What does this interface assume about me? What does it reward or discourage? What paths does it normalise or conceal?

One path to such awareness is *critical noticing*. This involves paying attention not just to the content one consumes, but to the contours of its delivery. Consider how Google's auto-suggestions complete thoughts before we've fully formed them, or how Spotify's algorithm reshapes musical identity by nudging listening habits. Platforms like TikTok reduce participation to a narrow loop of engagement: watch, like, scroll, repeat. Over time, this environment starts to *feel natural*, its rhythms internalised. But the fact that something feels intuitive doesn't mean it is neutral. Often, it means it has succeeded in encoding its logic into your behaviour.

To respond, individuals can begin developing personal interpretive frameworks. One such model is what philosopher Don Ihde termed "technological mediation"—the idea that technologies always come between us and the world, altering our perception and relation to it. Applied to daily life, this insight encourages users to consider how a tool mediates intention: Does the calendar app support reflection or overcommitment? Does the messaging platform invite genuine dialogue or demand perpetual responsiveness? These are not trivial considerations. *Small design choices compound into large behavioural patterns*. Recognising the mediation at work allows for intentional resistance or reconfiguration.

Some may argue that this kind of critical posture is too demanding—that constant vigilance in the face of design is exhausting. But the goal is not perpetual suspicion. Rather, it is to establish a rhythm of reflection. Not every scroll needs interrogation, but periodically asking, "Why did I end up here?" can reveal otherwise hidden dynamics. Over time, these questions build a form of cognitive posture—a muscle of mindful interaction that strengthens the user's sense of authorship within a system built to automate.

This orientation also implies a shift in values. In place of frictionless efficiency, the conscious user learns to value *deliberate slowness*. Not the slowness of delay, but of discernment. The friction of reading terms of service before accepting. The pause before sharing an article. The decision to leave a comment rather than simply reacting. Each moment of deliberation interrupts the automation of the interface. It *reclaims space* for meaning.

Yet conscious engagement isn't just about individual reflection. It's also about social coordination. Many of the most potent interfaces are social by design—collapsing public and private spheres, collapsing the distance between creation and consumption. To live consciously in such systems means not only interpreting design choices for oneself, but recognising their shared consequences. When a platform normalises surveillance (as with default GPS tracking), or erodes boundaries between work and life (as with Slack or Teams notifications), the effects are collective. Thus, *individual sovereignty depends on collective norms*. Conscious digital life must include conversations with peers, colleagues, and communities about what we accept, resist, or reshape together.

Interestingly, this awareness opens space for creative subversion. Artists, designers, and technologists have begun to reimagine digital engagement—not by abandoning systems, but by reconfiguring them. The browser extension 'Unfollow Everything' allows users to reclaim their Facebook feeds. Projects like 'Slow Social' experiment with platforms that delay posts to encourage reflection. Privacy-respecting services like Signal or ProtonMail invert the assumptions of data extraction. These alternatives demonstrate that living within designed systems doesn't mean accepting them as given. It means *negotiating their terms*—sometimes with critique, sometimes with hacks, sometimes with exit.

Ultimately, the goal is not perfect control, but *meaningful participation*. There is no clean boundary between user and system in today's digital life. What matters is the texture of engagement—the degree to which users feel able to exercise judgement, adjust their tools, and navigate complexity with eyes open. Consciously living within design means embracing partial agency. It means understanding that some aspects of the system will shape us, and choosing which ones we allow to do so.

There is a kind of maturity in this stance. It avoids both naïve techno-optimism and reactionary withdrawal. It accepts the inevitability of design while refusing its determinism. It holds that while you cannot control the system, *you can still choose how to relate to it*. And that choice, once recognised, is the seed of autonomy.

Futureproofing Agency

A world in which your refrigerator decides when you've run out of milk, your car negotiates traffic on your behalf, and your digital assistant quietly nudges your calendar to optimise productivity may sound like a technological utopia—but only if autonomy remains intact. The deeper our lives intertwine with ambient computing, AI companions, and context-aware systems, the less visible and more consequential the design of those systems becomes. *The core question is no longer just "What does this technology do?" but "Whose logic does it follow—and do I have any say in it?"* Futureproofing agency is not about resisting innovation. It's about ensuring the future doesn't quietly remove the need—or ability—to choose.

We tend to assume that progress moves in a linear fashion: from manual to automatic, from effort to ease, from command to delegation. But agency doesn't vanish in a dramatic rupture; it erodes subtly, outsourced by degrees to systems designed to be helpful. As more decisions are pre-handled by AI—what route we take, what media we consume, even how we emotionally respond—the risk is not that we will be controlled, but that we will stop noticing when we are being guided. The question of agency, then, must shift from how we assert our will in opposition to technology to how we *co-author* outcomes within it. *Preserving choice in the future requires learning to see choice in the present—even when it's obscured by convenience.*

Take, for example, AI companions—digital entities that simulate human conversation, offer companionship, and increasingly serve as emotional co-regulators. Their design raises serious questions not only about privacy or performance, but about psychological shaping. When a system is trained to optimise your comfort or engagement, does it reinforce your current preferences, challenge them, or subtly reshape them to serve the interests of its creators? These companions don't merely respond to you—they are engineered to steer you. If you're venting, are you being validated or redirected? If you're indecisive, are you being nudged toward a brand, a mood, a worldview? *The algorithms beneath the interface carry values. Understanding this isn't paranoia—it's literacy.*

Ambient computing introduces a more diffuse challenge. Unlike explicit interfaces—screens, menus, apps—the ambient layer blends into the environment: thermostats that adjust silently, speakers that anticipate your needs, notifications that surface only when "relevant." This seamlessness is often marketed as frictionless living. But when systems make decisions in the background, *interpretability suffers*. And without interpretability, accountability collapses. One cannot contest what one does not perceive. What disappears here is not power, but the *sightline to power*—the sense that something could be otherwise, or that you could intervene.

To futureproof agency, we must recalibrate our expectations of what responsible design looks like. Rather than tools that *handle* our choices invisibly, we need systems that *invite* our awareness deliberately. This is not a call for endless confirmation dialogues or user burden. It is a demand for interfaces that surface context, illuminate consequences, and respect the user's capacity for reflection. In high-stakes settings—like algorithmic hiring systems or automated lending decisions—this might mean offering audit trails and override mechanisms. In personal contexts—like AI-curated mental health apps—it could mean offering transparency into content generation and disclosing which data is being used to shape responses.

None of this is simply technical. It's cultural. The default mode of technology adoption today is passive assent. We install, accept, swipe, and scroll. But future agency will require a shift toward *consensual engagement*. This does not mean becoming paranoid or techno-suspicious. It means approaching systems with the same mental posture we bring to contracts, medicine, or legal advice: informed participation. The posture must be one of curiosity, not cynicism; of empowerment, not avoidance. The goal is not to become an engineer, but to be literate in the consequences of design—even when you didn't design the system yourself.

That brings us to the design of defaults. Default settings are among the most consequential decisions in technology, precisely because they frame the experience before the user knows they have options. In emerging systems—particularly those using reinforcement learning or generative modelling—defaults are often dynamic, adapting in real time based on user behaviour. This introduces a kind of *personalised inertia,* where the system optimises toward what it predicts you want, rather than what you consciously intend. While this can be useful in reducing cognitive load, it can also narrow the aperture of possibility. *What begins as a helpful shortcut can become an invisible cage.*

Some teams are beginning to design for intentional friction. For instance, some AI companions now include "reflection pauses" after emotionally charged conversations, inviting users to re-read or re-consider their statements before they're stored or acted on. Similarly, ambient systems in experimental smart homes allow users to visualise the logic behind a change—like why a light dimmed or a thermostat adjusted—making the invisible visible. These examples are not mainstream yet, but they signal a different design philosophy: one that treats the user not merely as a consumer of outputs, but as a collaborator in outcomes.

Education will be critical. Agency can't be outsourced. In a world of intelligent environments and synthetic assistants, we must cultivate cognitive skills once assumed to be obsolete—discernment, patience, critical interpretation. Even the simple question *"Why did this just happen?"* is a powerful act of reclaiming perspective. Futureproofing doesn't require rejecting tools; it requires refusing to be absorbed by them uncritically. *Autonomy in a designed world is not an inheritance—it is a skill.*

The final dimension is legal and regulatory. As AI systems become more entangled in core social infrastructures—healthcare, finance, education—the legal conception of agency must evolve too. This includes clearer definitions of consent, stronger rights to explanation, and mechanisms for redress. But personal agency cannot wait on policy. It must be practised now, in the margins of everyday interaction. The way you set up a new device, the questions you ask your digital assistant, the permissions you grant an app—these are not trivialities. They are rehearsals for the future.

The architectures we inhabit tomorrow are being shaped today. Whether those architectures amplify our volition or attenuate it depends not only on the ethics of engineers or the vigilance of regulators, but on the awareness and habits of users. *To futureproof agency is not to resist design, but to demand design that respects the human will—even when that will is fallible, unfinished, or evolving.* Technology will continue to grow more ambient, more persuasive, more predictive. But agency—if we choose to practise it—can grow stronger, too.

About the Author

Rowan Hale writes at the intersection of technology, ethics, and everyday systems. With a deep curiosity about how design and infrastructure shape human behavior, Hale explores the quiet forces behind what feels like free choice—from the routes we drive to the information we trust. Known for turning invisible mechanics into vivid insight, Hale invites readers to question the defaults built into modern life. In Reprogrammed, Hale continues a mission to reveal how convenience technologies subtly redraw the lines of agency, offering readers the tools to navigate an increasingly pre-decided world with intention and clarity.

www.ingramcontent.com/pod-product-compliance
Lightning Source LLC
Chambersburg PA
CBHW031340230926
51848CB00002B/312
9789371779456